Move

Live in the Full

Bill Huyett

Kindle Direct Publishing
04/02/2019

visit **Amazon Books**
ISBN-13: 978-1794452794
Imprint: Independently published

Second Edition
05/28/2020

Table of Contents

Chapter 1

Birth of the "Move To Empty"

Spiritual struggles and searching

Who will understand this?
The world will see this as weak.
My family will see this as weak.
There is no other way for me.

I still haven't found God, so maybe
I should just wait for the moment I am found.

Breathe in, breathe out.

Move to Empty Emerges

Moving through life events.
Family, work, faith, and fun.
Upswings and downturns,
joys and sorrows in full.

My ego in full control,
with mind-based reality
and undervalued spirit,
hidden messages in place.

God's of humility begin
to speak in bold expressions,
but my ego remains confident,
laughing in the face of truth.

Coincidence?
Science. Facts.
And yet, God's speak with
repeated strikes to the ego heart.

What message can this be?
The invisible God has no strength.
I look, the formulas are not there.
I search in dogmas empty coffins.

Writing describes my travels.
Poetry describes my journey,
my struggles are apparent
and my lack of insight abounds.

Light breaks through the cracks.
A new path discovered with
humility guiding the way.
It's time to empty, to become small.

A Mystical Journey Begins

I ignore the challenge given my charge.
I fall, fall again all too willingly.
Searching for help but I cannot see
the gift, the gift of a peaceful destiny.

An intellectual, or so I might think.
I see the Gift as a story for the weak,
some other answer that I must seek.
There must be more, but it eludes me now.

How many times must I travel this road?
I look at my reflection, it does not change.
Still the grays, dark shadows so strange.
The goal is plain to see, but I do not change.

Why do I long for this change, why me?
Was the pattern engraved in my childhood?
Where does the battle begin for evil and good?
Why can't I see the sign, it eludes me now.

Why can't I believe, I cannot find God.
Why can't I accept, I long for peace.
The pain, the pain of loneliness will not cease.
I pray, but who am I praying to, I pray.

Don't want to accept because there's nothing else,
conditioned to utilize only my mind.
My heart, if only I could let my heart find
what my mind cannot reach, my spirit could embrace.

Why is my heart so hard to faith?
Human nature is a circle of doom.
I am blind and this cloud continues to loom.
I can only pray for the door to open soon.

Searching for a way, it's so hard to relate.
The times have changed man forever.
The new science works hard to severe.
The path has been covered, I cannot see.

Who Am I

Who am I that I am given this quest
to want a relationship with God?

Who am I to be given an answer,
to be given knowledge and wisdom
concerning this relationship?

However, somehow, I sense some kind of
a pull, some kind of longing,
and maybe, some kind of direction
towards an answer.

For this I am thankful.

Dream Message

A had a dream last night, do not know why.
Falling at the cross, a large living cross.
I couldn't control myself, I felt very lost.
I was so lonely, just cried and cried.

The darkness, the sorrow all around.
The only light, the light coming from the cross.
That cross, trying to look at that cross,
but the smoke in my eyes would not let me see.

Kneeling in the church, hands pressed to my face.
The tears of sorrow continuing to flow.
Trying to hide, not wanting anyone to know.
Not willing to open and receive the Lord.

When I awoke, I didn't remember this dream,
but as the day went on it came back to me.
What is the meaning, is God talking to me?
I'm still confused, I'm blind to the truth.

Blind In Faith

O God of human emotion.
A cry not of doubt but of weak faith.
O invisible God, why don't I see?
Why hold my blindness against me?

Why does human logic go against you?
Why give your creature a lack of sight?
This is not a question of you O invisible God
but of my lack of wisdom and insight.

Why does the gift of Faith evade me?
How does one pray to an invisible God?
How does one ask when the answer
can either come as a yes or a no?

Earthly knowledge
builds a wall
between
Science and Faith.

Shaken

Foggy vision blurs the start.
In a strange room, dimly lit.
Mother yells, Jesus is at the door
and He wants to talk to me.

Cold steel feeling inside.
Blood dripping from my nose
into a bowl on the counter.
Not ready, not prepared.

Blood now in my hands.
All the things I have done.
What will I say, what will I do?
Not ready, not prepared.

Shaken from the message in the dream.
Awake, staring at shadows in the room.
Mind searching for an explanation.
Heart aching from the guilty plea.

Travels to Empty

I am nothing.
I have nothing.
I am nothing but God's child and that is everything.
God is stripping me down.

No one will understand this.
The world will never understand this.
I was created imperfect.
In this world I will always be imperfect.

Only when totally united with God will I become whole.
I am nothing.
Move to empty. God will fill the empty.
The more I have emptied the more room for God to fill.

No one to talk to, no one will understand.
Even in this, I have nothing.
I do not understand, and I am not understood.
All pride and ego must be emptied.

Who will understand this?
The world will see this as weak.
My family will see this as weak.
There is no other path for me.

Travels to Empty (notes)

I have discovered that this move to empty may not happen in one big jump. The Ego or self has layers. I have moved a layer down. I have recognized the top layer of self (maybe this layer and all layers are different for each person). For me, it was the delusion of self-importance. This travel to empty is a journey. There will be moving forward and maybe sometimes backward. As I write this it may seem as if I have chosen this journey. I have not. As a matter of fact, my ego does not like it at all. This first layer requires acts of humility. These acts may be self-imposed but in my case, they are imposed by outside forces. I have been continually reminded of my inadequacies. At first, I was defensive and angry. Then I felt depressed. As I slowly begin to accept this reality it is amazing the varied glimpses and insights I am having concerning my experiences in life. A slight feeling of joy springs up at the recognition of the beauty (inner) and talent of others. My renewed interest in writing has helped me to express this journey.

A Quiet Walk (Spiritual Moments)

Noble oaks and maples.
Manicured lawn and paths.
Names carved on stone markers.
Memories of those from our past.

A tradition lost on the old and lonely.
The young seldom step on this sacred soil.
Crosses, statues, symbols provide consolation
or perhaps a simple display of respect.

Plants and flowers decorate and honor.
Flags wave and salute heroes from long ago.
Those claiming a moment in time
weaving in and out of our lives.

Monuments for both the rich and the poor,
the attractive and the ugly,
the old and sometimes the young.
All of these returned to simple dust.

The sun shines on each without prejudice.
The wind treats all with equality.
Mother earth accepts everyone.
Born with nothing, return with the same.

Still Searching

Who am I to want to know the things of great minds?
Who am I to want to think thoughts far too deep
for me to provide answers?

Is there a Creator,
or are we some grand accident,
some random freak of nature?

If we are here through random evolution
then we have no purpose, no reason for being.
Science is a tool, a method for discovery.
Science does not provide a purpose,
just a means of getting there.
Science is a digging tool, not the treasure.

How do we explain thought itself?
How do we explain Reason?
How do we explain love?
How do we explain self-awareness?

A Simple Prayer

God, please be part of my life.
I ask of my own free will.
Please send your Spirit
to move in me.

I am an average man
who makes my own world complex.
Please help me simplify.

God, please be a part of my life.
I do not understand religion.
I do not understand Faith.
However, I do have hope
and I try to share love.
Please send your Spirit
to move in me.

Joy and Sadness

So much good in my life.
So much to be thankful for.
Yet still the trials and tribulations
try to take center stage,
and sometimes they succeed.

It is hard sometimes
to rejoice at the greatness of the boat
when the leaks keep wearing me down.

The trials and tribulations are not
necessarily the problem, it is
the feeling that there are no solutions,
no way of making things better.

Where are Peace and Joy?

Declaration of Self

I've been given the gift of insight,
and the curse of not being able to change things.

I've been given the desire to be perfect
and the abilities to make many, many mistakes.

My job puts me on the peak of a mountain
with success or failure just one slip away.

I really don't mind competition,
I just can't stand to lose.

I know I have a lot to offer.
Why are my inabilities so often pointed out?

I know I have a good attitude
but it so often gets beaten down.

I live in a world that demands you push hard
and I have a heart that wants peace and quiet.

I've been given two children to teach how to live,
and yet have no clue of what the hell I'm doing.

I have many responsibilities and obligations
and they create a very large trap.

I know I'm different than the image
I'm trying to create.

I know I'm different then what I
perceive others think I should be.

I know I have very many blessings.
Then why am I unhappy?

My life is a world of paradox
and sometimes it just gets the best of me.

I feel I have no way to change things
and now my body and mind hurt.

I Have Thought Much

I have thought much but I have learned nothing.
I have done much but accomplished little.
I have noticed much, but grown only some.
I have searched much, but have found only pieces.

I will wait, I will be still.
For I have looked, but have not found.
I can only rest, for I am empty.
I have found nothing to fulfill.

But no, I am still not empty,
for I am not pure.
Not in some kind of righteous religious pure,
but pure to self, pure to others, pure to God.

How can I expect to find God near?
This is not a "time to beat me down" statement
but a recognition of a lack of focus or intention.
I will wait, I will be still.

My Soul

I have laid open my soul,
wide open for everyone to see.
I have exposed my true self.
I have realized there's nothing else I can be.

I have shown that I do not have all the answers.
I have shown how far away I am from the ideal.
Perhaps surprised some who thought I had something
more than my humanness and poor words of how I feel.

Some have laughed and made fun.
Some have picked all the meat from the bone.
Even those closest and most trusted
have shown that I am open and alone.

I have learned to accept who I am,
and maybe still have a few tricks up my sleeve.
There will be many who will be left disappointed,
probably few who I will get to believe.

But there is a great strength in truth to self.
There is freedom from guilt and false desire.
The crushing weight of trying to please others,
replaced by love of life, lifting myself higher.

Experiencing Move to Empty

What does one say when there aren't any words?
No words to express thoughts.
No words to discuss ideas.
Words in books fall short of any meaning.

All molds, all categories fall away.
Man's attempts to define and create dogma,
platitudes and cliches, weak human attempts
to use words, not actions to be kind.

What is religion, if it's only words?
A relationship with Spirit, with God
is not through words, rules or dogma.
It is, as God is, limitless and
beyond imagination. The created mind,
the human mind cannot express this,
cannot teach this.

So what do I say, what should I read?
Who can teach me? It is an awareness of
self-being, self-existence, in a world
so unimaginable. Our senses do not
work here. Our human interaction with
each other is so flawed, so weak.
However, we are called to bring this
being of love to each other.

So what do I do, how should I act?
What should I say, what should I write?

When one's being, one's existence is so small,
so insignificant, yet our awareness alone of
the possible relationship is the most significant
evidence that we do matter, we are important.

Balance

Well, things are as they are.
I have lived some, learned some, grown some,
lost some, hurt some, loved some.
Perhaps the secret is to expect little,
to live in the present,
leaving the past for historians
and the future to the gypsies.

I still haven't found God, so maybe
I should just wait for the moment I am found.

I have learned a little about myself.
I breathe, I think, I feel
and somehow I am aware of these three
parts that I think might be my spirit.

So for now, I feel content in my journey.
I will become still, become quiet.

Empty

Alone.
You are a tree growing in an empty field.
A river persevering through a desert.

Alone.
When you are faced with hard decisions.
At the final call, when a choice has to be made.

Alone.
You are a mountain eroding from the winds of doubt.
You are a dark alley, poorly lit with end unknown.

Alone.
When your fears hover above with their pressing weight.
Responsibilities cage you in preventing release.

Alone.
You are a sapling growing among oaks and redwoods.
A grain of sand facing an angry sea.

Alone.
When a judgement is thrust upon you, your soul lies bare.
Pick up the broken pieces and try to rebuild.

Alone.
You are a sinner, human in every way.
A shattered sculpture, mistakes follow you every day.

Alone.
When you are misunderstood and cast aside.
You are ugly, unaccepted for your beauty within.

Alone.
The world is going where you can't follow.
You are a foreigner in a harsh and dirty land.

Alone.
What you thought was solid, you know must soon change.
Your heart is tearing, but you know you must let go.

Alone.
You are a fortress, although inside you are very fragile.
You are an egg, hard shell, life pulsing inside.

Alone.
You are a seed, buried beneath the cold snow.
Waiting for Spring to explode through and bring new life.

Recognize the Present

In trying to recognize the present,
the world displayed all around me,
I have felt moments of joy.
This joy came from noticing the
beauty, the wonders jumping out
from my surroundings.
I have been and continue to be blessed.

However, I have so far to go with my
relationships with others.
I am still easily frustrated and hurt.
Zen tells me not to ignore these feelings,
but to recognize them, then to let them
pass and move off into the past.

Listening Prayer

Listening, listening, listening.
Listening without speaking.
Listening without giving an opinion.
Listening without giving analysis.
Listening without saying a word.
Putting on a face of compassion
and understanding.

Breaking Through

Where is true nature?
Where is Divine liberty?
Caught in a journey
not of my own making.
But yes, my own making.

Is it only my selfish will
that desires a different road?
Am I confused about this
unique call in the night?
It has become very strong.

I am caught on a track racing
forward. Loud voices, hectic
schedules made by those
seeking greater profits and
greater busyness. I am tired.

The gift I've been given,
insight into another truth,
perhaps just a self-illusion,
but this time it seems real,
this time it hasn't dissolved.

This call is pulling me apart.
My move to empty has not
lead to an expected destination.
This journey inside has uncovered
layers and years of clouded sight.

This is not to say that my life
has not had joy and blessings.
No husband or father could be
more blessed than I have been.
This call is transforming my soul.

This call has changed my sight.
The blind will truly see, shackles
falling away, light shining through.
However, the ego has built strong
walls, a fortress tall and protected.

The struggle continues on,
battle lines being drawn.
The ego is cunning and clever.
It has worked hard to be this
comfortable and established.

The Master has used a secret door.
The Light has broken through,
my heart is yours to transform,
though I reach out wounded,
I'm falling in love, time for a change.

My trust is in you Lord, lead me.
My hope is in you Lord, guide me.
My faith is in you Lord, protect me.
My life is in you Lord, love me.
Wisdom come to me. Amen, Amen

God Is Like

What might God be like for me?

God is like good memories, the kind that catch
you off guard and make your heart surge.

God is like that moment when the thought flashes
through your mind about how amazing and special
every second of this life is.

God is like that feeling you get when you know
you haven't been a good friend,
but God wants to be your friend anyway.

God is like that moment when you're in awe of nature.
God is like hope in something better.

Purposeless Purpose

The purposeless purpose?
Living life in the moment
with the realization that the
miracle comes in small glimpses.

The miracle of life is
bursting open all around us,
silently screaming, here I am.
The purpose is not only to notice
but to rejoice with awe and gratitude.

Let our thoughts, words, and actions
be a reflection and respectfulness
of these simple but wonderful blessings.

Rest

Rest.

Breathe and take notice.

Breathe in, breathe out.

You cannot breathe the past or the future, only the present.

Breathe in, breathe out.

Chapter 2
Silent Whispers, Quiet Inspirations

The Ego Discovered
Being Present
Being awake to Moments

*Be the voice of encouragement. If this is your only gift, you
can change the world*

I am here with an open heart, please transform me

Perhaps the Artists

Perhaps the artists are the special ones.
Perhaps they have found a way to break through,
found a way to connect this trial life with real life.
Perhaps they sense the real,
only to realize that we are the expression of God.
Maybe, too, the writers and philosophers know.
Maybe they see the real.

The Chapel

This room is a special room and it will always be special for it has helped bring me to this point, but this room cannot contain the amazing vastness and Glory that is God. This immense creative force cannot be contained or confined in any way, for it is everywhere and everything. And yet, God is also in the smallest of things, the building blocks of all things. God is the life force. God is the creative action, continuously bringing new life from all things, even death.

"Be welcoming"

"Show them.
Show them what life in Christ is like.
Why worry about things you can't change?
Why worry about things you don't understand?
Live in the present.
Put your hope in me.
Live it. Then you will see."

Here I am Lord. What can I do for you?
"Show them."

"Teach them."

Teach them what? My faith is weak.

"Teach them about my heart, it's mercy and love"

"I Am.
Trust me in all things.
Let go of all lesser things.
Trust me. Give yourself to me.
Trust me, even if you don't understand"

Love By The Moments

Love by the moments.
Love in the moments.

I went deep into prayer.
I allowed my "self" to get smaller and smaller, focusing on humility. It is not about me, but it is about me in a way you wouldn't think.

We are completely loved by God, and as we accept this love, we know that we are as special as we can be. Again, love is dynamic, always in the form of giving and sacrificing. God's love is always complete, always what we need. We love God by opening our heart. Then we need to turn and be a conduit of God's love to others.

The smaller our ego becomes, the greater God can love us. The smaller I became the more the Spirit was present (not like an apparition, but like an awareness, confidence). The more I let go, the more I felt like I was being held.

I felt at peace. I felt light. I felt unburdened. I felt subtly surprised because I didn't expect this experience. I was just trying to be present and open. This was not mystical, it just felt good, nice. I was aware of all my faults, maybe more aware than usual. I was thinking about how I can change some of these not-so-nice human habits, what I can do to change my unloving nature. This is when I had the thought of "love by moments". This experience didn't last long, but I really didn't want to leave to go back to work. It just felt really nice.

Notice

Notice the moment.
Notice your breathing.
Notice the life inside of you.
Notice the life outside of you.
Notice the gentle breeze touching your skin.
Notice the warmth of the sun.
Notice the plants, trees, birds, bugs,
all in the life of creation.
Notice the people, their faces, their voices,
their movements and words.
All part of the dynamic body of life around you.
This is where you find God. Learn to notice.

Love

Embrace love, because it's in your heart.
The happiness, joy, the feeling of being loved by God,
the peace that this gives you,
the confidence that this gives you,
the feeling of freedom from a heavy yoke
that your previous understanding of God imposed.
This is the good news!

Tell others about what is in your heart.
Be authentic.
What this means is that you don't have to worry
about how to explain your new relationship with God.
You don't have to use wordy,
intellectual, biblical explanations.
Just be authentic with what's in your heart.
Let love shine through.

Choose to Love

Choose to love in the moments.
In the busy moments, love.
In the quiet moments, love.

In the moments at work, love.
There is no reason to act differently at work.
Be the face of love, all connected.

Make work holy. Be a blessing to others.
Be fair and honest. Be friendly and welcoming.
This is a chance to bring God to others.

All moments are opportunities.
Be a presence of the living God.
Open yourself to allow the Spirit to act through you.

Be open, be ready.
You don't know when the Spirit will act.
Be always open.

This gift that I've been given,
this great love and friendship with the Spirit,
is the cause for great joy in my heart.

It gives me peace. It makes me smile.
It supports my daily life.
This great gift is my true self.

The Kingdom (Part One)

In the Kingdom, time and space are irrelevant.
There is only now. There is no before death and after death.
There is only present, presence.
Death has already been conquered.
Yes, there is still the physical death,
and this is perhaps what is needed
to finally separate some of us from our ego.
But our spiritual ego-death can happen before our physical
death, allowing us to experience the Kingdom now.
Rebirth has already been completed.
The self is gone. New life in Union has been born.

I have been shaken.
I have been stunned.
At the moment, I have no words to describe this message.
I'm having some difficulty even absorbing it.
As I looked at the crucifix, it seemed lost in time, or,
that time didn't exist.
It seemed like I was simply present,
with the future losing meaning because everything was now.
Something about this moment seemed very real and true.
It will be an experience to think about for some time.
Amazingly, this removes our physical death as the end thing,
but establishes it as simply a transition point.
As a human being, that changes everything.
This removes the power from death.
It removes death as the definition of the last thing,
by removing it from the sequence of time.

(Part Two)

My work is to reflect light.
My work is to be a channel for love,
to be a mirror of love.
My way is to be open,
to be transformed by the Spirit.

Everything seems to look different now.
The sky looks immense. It looks timeless.
It looks separate, like looking into something
so deep, so free.
It seems living, like a presence.
It seems full.

The chapel seems different.
My view of these objects has changed.
My understanding of them has changed,
knowing that they're symbols of something eternal.
Small parts of something real, but endless.

I am here, and not here.
I am there, and not there.
I am present.
There is before, now, and future.
Time is real, but only in the present.

All part of the whole,
I am both physical and spiritual.
Just as all things physical are temporary,
all things spiritual are eternal,
all connected with the one creative force.

Relationship

This relationship is an interaction with the Creator.
We receive love, and are nourished,
then allow this love to flow outward.

This action is transformative for us.
We are filled with joy
in the participation in this relationship.

Receiving and giving.
Receive grace, sharing grace.
This is the creative action, the creative force.

We open our heart to receive love,
and keep it open to give love.
In this way, we are on the path to union.
In this way, we are acting as a mirror of compassion.

Wonder of Creation

The wonder of creation is all around us.
It's in the air that we breathe.
It's inside you and outside of you.

Shake off the chains from your past.
Break away the blinders on your eyes.
Knock down the walls you've put around your heart.

Let go. Let go. Let go.
Fall completely into the arms of Love.
Allow the joy to consume you.

Come and live.
Come to the banquet and be fully nourished.
Open and accept.

One God

There is only one God, one Creator,
one perfect source of love,
available to all now and forever.

This is the "Good News".
All we need to do is open our heart,
accept and allow this amazing relationship to happen.

Humankind has been experiencing this relationship
in many ways since the beginning of time. One source,
unlimited and not bound by human understanding.

We need to let go,
just as we are,
and discover our true self.

Be filled with joy, peace. Smile, let it break through.
No rules, no deeds, just an open heart, open to this gift.
Where there is love, there is God.

When I Am Small

When I am small,
when I do the smallest thing with compassion,
it can grow bigger than can be imagined.
Trust the power of love.

My work is to marvel at the beauty in this world,
to marvel at the beauty of creation,
the creative action all around me,
especially in my fellow humankind.

My work is to be a beacon of hope,
a testament to faith,
witness to love in action,
all without applying the burden of my words.

Love in the moments.
The smile.
The simple hello.
The simple good morning, how are you?
The kind word.
The small encouragement.
The simple hug.
Being friendly.
Taking an interest, being a good listener, being genuine.
Offer your full attention (mentally, emotionally, physically).
Offer your patience.
Offer your understanding.
Presenting the Spirit to others.

The Gift

This Gift.
The Goal.
This Treasure.
The Way.

Love enduring forever.
Faith, hope, love.
Perfect love.
Perfect union.

Our unknowing.
Our struggles.
Our blindness
The flame is still there.

Perhaps not loved.
Perhaps abandoned.
Perhaps neglected.
The flame is still there.

Our intelligence.
Perhaps too logical.
Perhaps too proud.
The flame is still there.

Perhaps a broken promise.
Perhaps a broken heart.
Perhaps betrayed.
The flame is still there.

Perhaps survival.
Perhaps no choices.
Perhaps you're alone.
The flame is still there.

The night speaks with a voice not heard at any other time.
The quiet darkness speaks when we are silent.

Nighttime Prayer

The blessings are deep.
Love is deeper still.
Amazement.
Worthy, not worthy, this matters not.
Chosen child.
Beloved child.
Redeemed child.
Imperfect, but loved by Perfection.
Incomplete, but made whole by perfect love.
Empty, but made to overflow with unending compassion.

Deserved, not deserved, this matters not.
No more guilt, even if I feel guilty.
No more despair, even if I feel hopeless.
No more beating myself up, even if I feel wretched.
I am loved and accepted by the Creator of all things.
I am considered valuable to the
Source of all beautiful things.
I accept this love.
I am open.
Let me now be a conduit of this love to all.
Accepted as I am on a journey to union with the One.

To admire nature is a blessing and a gift.
Humans are very much part of nature,
although they try very hard to hide this fact,
as if somehow they were apart from it, not connected.
Our very life and death is a continuous display of this
inescapable relationship.

Science and Faith are no longer enemies.

The First

The First.
Relational energy.
Giving energy.
Being-presence-energy.
Matter-body, incarnation.
Spirit-relationship-perfect giving.

Creation.
Big bang.
An outward, giving explosion.
Expanding out in all directions.
Everything still part of the First.
Giving all of self.
Given with freedom.
Given with hope.
Giving without control.

Creation is an act of giving.
Creation is a giving of self to relationship
so relationship will give back to the Creator (the First).

The First gives but does not try to control.

The purpose of this life is the growing/developing of the freely given possibility of unity-relationship with the First.
Creation is the act of giving away of self with the chance of it not coming back.
It is the action (verb) of relationship.

The act of Faith is the act of allowing, the act of giving, the act of acceptance. All of which is completely void of control.

Initially, we empty ourselves.
Then we open ourselves, offer ourselves, and allow the Spirit to fill us and be fully present. We place our trust in love.
We give up the need and desire to control things.
We move with humility knowing from whom our source of guidance and joy comes.
Then, we mirror this presence outward.

> Empty.
> Open.
> Offer.
> Allow.
> Trust.
> Humility.
> Mirror.
> Rejoice.

This is the process of transformation.
This is the process of joining.

Not by Your Way

Not by your way.
Not by your time.
Give it up. Give up control.

Not by your own will.
Be open. Simply open your heart.
Accept love, not because of anything you've done.

You are special because of the Creators act of love.
Be open, allow this love to transform you,
transforming you by moving you toward union.

We can barely understand this.
We can only be open.
It seems too good to be true.
Be open. Simply open your heart.

Come With Me

Come with me to a place of gratitude.

Grateful for a loving Presence.
Grateful to be cradled in the arms of love.
Grateful to be a witness to the wonders
and mysteries of creation.
Grateful to be judged through the eyes
of mercy and compassion.
Grateful to be loved as I am.
Grateful to not only be included but actually
desired by God.
Grateful for the love that only wants
what is best for me.
Grateful to not have to accomplish special deeds
or acts to be loved, but simply to accept being loved.
Grateful to a God who loves all of creation
so much that He incarnates himself to be with us.

Come with me to a place of gratitude.

Selfless

Seek union with creation and the Creator.

Selflessness opens and empties us.
Creator-Love fills us.
Selflessness allows the flow, in and out,
of the Creator-Love.

Getting and giving. Flow.
Allowing rejoining, returning, reunion.

A selfless person does not use others.
A selfless person loves unconditionally.
A selfless person does not use others for self-satisfaction.
A selfless person loves by giving themselves to others.
A selfless person has relationships made of emptying
themselves and pouring out love-flow to others.

Share

Blessed with much, blessed with little, we share in love.

Hard life or easy life, we share in love.

Understood or misunderstood, we share in love.

Wanted or unwanted, we share in love.

Accepted or manipulated, we share in love.

Respected or disdained, we share in love.

A wise man or simple man, we share in love.

Supported or alone, we share in love.

During our labors or in free time, we share in love.

Like a mirror, we receive light and then reflect light.

We do not hoard the love we receive from God,

but empty ourselves,

and give freely what we received freely.

Blessings flow in, blessings flow out.

Strengthened by God, supported by Grace.

Love flows in, gratefulness flows out.

God Of Love

God of love.
God of life.
God of life source.
God of beauty.
God of creation.
God of the dynamic universe.
God of transformation.
God of giving.
God of forgiving.
God of sacrifice.
God of incarnation.
God of wonder.
One God.
God the source.
God the reality.
God the energy.
God the everything.
God the everywhere.
God of flow.
God of all unity.
God of all love.

No Separation

There is no separation.
We are all human beings,
all part of the same creation.
The only separations
between us are man-made.
These separations come from
our different understandings
of our meaning or purpose.
The separation comes from
our lack of understanding
that we are all one,
that we are all created as one
and we are one with the Holy Spirit.
Until we understand that the separations
are of our own creation we will remain divided.
So I believe that true religion
is based on being one and being together
and joining in this search
for purpose and meaning.
I believe that in the end
it's all based on unity and love.
We are all just human beings
trying to pursue truth and meaning
and purpose for our lives,
but in the end, we are all just
a common people all trying
to achieve the same thing,
all trying to feel loved.

The Spirit is a specialist in transformation. But, sometimes we are transformed through suffering. Stay strong and joyful and open.

Pain

Perhaps the sky must be gray for a while.
Maybe pain must make a visit.
Hopefully, it will not stay long.

It could be a big transition point is near.
Be with me Spirit of life.
If I am not ready, please fill the void.

May humility be my guide.
May compassion be my strength.
Hold me up where I may fall.

I will embrace hope.
I will trust my heart
for the strength to carry on.

Spiritual Solitude

Spiritual solitude is the realization that nothing or nobody or no action can satisfy that which can only be satisfied by Love.

And yet, perhaps once we've been through the tunnel of purification which burns away our reliance on people and things for our self-worth, we will become aware of our true connection to the very people and things we are searching for.

Maybe someday this facade, this masquerade, this emptiness, this pain and longing, these motions dedicated to perpetuating pointless busyness will give way to my true purpose, my true self. Maybe someday the clouds will clear, the smoke dissipate, and the beauty of my soul will be free to live in the Eden that was prepared for me from the beginning of time, existing in union with the fullness of Being.

Until then I will breathe, I will endure, I will wait and watch for those glimpses of the simpleness and magnificence that are granted in moments of Grace. And when my body stumbles and falls, let me hold tight to the mystical Spirit presence, carrying me through each day toward peaceful unity.

This Experience of God

This experience of God is so beautiful, peaceful and real.
It is truly all around you and inside you.
It is in the fabric of every moment.
It is woven so closely with all we experience
that we almost surely miss it.
We look everywhere and still don't see.
We are blind to what is gloriously being displayed.
We cry out that we want to see God all the while missing the
very presence in all things and everywhere.
The problem is we project our idea of what God should be on
all things, creating blinders that prevent our spiritual sight.
We project our will and our ego,
disbelieving the experience of the real, true God.
Our expectations, desires, and longings for the God we want
prevents us from seeing the God that we need.
Be still. Breathe in and breathe out. Let go.
Seeing God does not start on the outside,
but starts on the inside.
Once you can break down your internal barriers,
then you will also begin to see God outside,
in everyone and everything.
God is in the real.
God is in life, in our joys and sorrows,
in our sufferings and ecstasies, and everywhere in between.
This life is about transformation.
Transformation of our mind, body, and spirit,
all leading to our union with the One.
Our transformation must happen in our heart.
The senses will then open which will flood our mind and spirit
with the presence of the living God, the God of every moment,
the God of beauty, peace, love.
Empty yourself, and be filled with the God of all.

Vessel

I am simply a vessel,
with infinite spirit outside, infinite spirit inside,
all the while connected to my incarnate body.
I was created in the image of the Creator.

Through Grace, I'm connected to the flow.
No time or boundaries here.
All connected to all,
nothing to create divisions.

Nothing to defend.
No death, because I've already died to self.
It is all gift here.
Emptiness and complete fullness.
The Paradox of Unity.

The Amazing

The Amazing is hidden in plain sight.
Let the scales fall from your eyes.
It's in everything and everywhere.
It's hidden in the atom.
It's hidden in the universe.
It's hidden in nature.
It's hidden in acceptance.
It's hidden in offering.
It's hidden in forgiveness.
It's felt in contentment and peace.
It's felt in loving action.
It's felt in the creative force.
It's felt in suffering.
It's felt in our failing.
It's felt in mercy.
It's felt in transformation.
It's felt in union with the One.
This is the Kingdom.
Let God give you sight.
Let God set you free.
Open yourself to Amazing Grace.

Busy Moments

In the busy moments, love.
Even when your mind is racing,
when you are having trouble concentrating,
bring your mind back to love.

In those small gaps, the ones in between all of those other
thoughts, are great opportunities to bring back love. This is
how we keep our relationship with the Spirit present in our
daily life. A continuous recognition and acknowledgment of
who gives us life.

Also, even though these are only brief moments, the reminder
of our living God can be very uplifting and change your whole
attitude. It brings a smile to your face and confidence to bear
with joy.

Praying without words,
even when you can't form the words or thoughts,
by bringing your mind back to love.
It's always there, and it will fill the void.

Prayer to the Spirit

Holy Spirit,
help to remove anything between us.

No roadblocks.
No barriers.
Nothing that I create.
Nothing that others create.
Not doctrine.
Not religion.
Not words, thoughts, deeds.
Not teachers and preachers.
Not Tradition.
Not a Book.
Not my desire for understanding.
Not my desires at all.
Let me become spiritually dead,
so I can be resurrected to new spiritual life.
Let nothing act as a barrier to Truth.
Let me live with total openness.
Let me always have an open heart,
always open to the journey towards Unity.

Silence

Silence.
When we are silent,
free from all noise and distraction,
we can hear God speak to us in our heart,
not through words,
not through thoughts,
but through our open heart,
through spirit connection.

Every moment offers an opportunity
to allow love to flow through us.
Every breath.
Through all our senses.
Through every relationship and encounter.

Speak With Love

Speak with love, not words.
Preach with love, not words.
Act with love, not words.
Pray with love, not words.
Love always.

Why Me

I do not understand.
How is it that You love me?
How is it possible?
How can this be?

Out of millions of stars,
a universe far and wide.
Thousands of millions of years.
Thousands of millions of miles.

How did You find me?
All the noise, all the commotion.
You come in the quiet.
Silently, a gentle reflection.

A tear then tears slowly fall.
A thought, my heart stirs.
A slight gasp, You are here.
No words, subtle peace occurs.

Profound humility.
How is it that You love me?
How is it possible?
How can this be?

A love beyond understanding.
Head bowed low, heart open wide.
Wrapped in warmth, spirit aglow.
Stay with me Presence divine.

Tears now running freely.
Holy One touching my soul.
Caressing, transforming.
Once broken, now becoming whole.

Silent, still, empty and full.
Hope reaching beyond impossible.
How is it that You love me?
A love received, Grace fulfilled.

Ancient Wisdom, time and before time.
Ancient Word, now and before then.
Ancient Source, infinite light, and love.
Amen.

Speak Less

Be joyful. Bring joy outward.
Be a servant to others.
Be a support to others.
Selfless. Humble. Present.
Be silent.
Be silent as much as possible.
Words are not better than silence.
Be quiet. Be silent.
No more reading spiritual "how to" books.
Listen to the Spirit instead.
Let the Spirit guide you.
Be patient. Be quiet.
Be joyful. Bring joy outward.
Selfless. Humble. Present.

Sometimes, the night is like a voice crying out in the wilderness.

In The Night It Is Silent

In the night, it is silent.
    We can think slowly, clearly.
    The senses rest, but the spirit soars.
    No need for spoken words.
    No need to impress.
    No one placing judgments.
    We whisper prayers to the One.
    We reflect on true self.
In the night, we ask for mercy and love.
    Our memory both cries and sings.
    We are aware of love.
    We smile from our heart.
    We see our blessings more keenly.
    We receive healing.
    We are transformed.
    We are humble.
    We give thanks.
    We find peace.
    We can think slowly, clearly.
In the night, it is silent.

Where Are You

Spirit, where are you, where did you go?

I Am here.
Do not look with your eyes or listen with your ears.
Search with your heart. Open your heart.
I Am in the darkness.
I Am in every moment and every place
bursting with energy and life and love.
I Am in your every breath.
Breathe in and breathe out, I Am there.
You look here and there with blind eyes.
You think you have lost me. You think I have gone.
You're like a tiny child who quickly becomes
scared when he thinks his father is gone.
You do not understand My ways and My being.
You do not understand the Spirit of life and creation.
You still think you are separate from Me,
somehow drifting alone in space.
You do not know that in order to have any understanding
you must let go of what you think.
You get lost in the false importance of the matters of this world.
You grasp at a reality that you think you control,
but this is not true reality.
True reality exists in moments of love.
Do not cling to some notion that there
is a darkness separate from Me.
There is nowhere you can go where I Am not there,
waiting for you with endless love.
I will never abandon you.

Even in the moments when you feel the most darkness,
when your mind has tricked you into thinking you are alone
and lost, I Am cradling you in My arms, I Am holding you in My
heart and immersing you in a love beyond your
comprehension.
Relax and let go, fall into peace. I Am here.

Candle

I am a paradox
in which brokenness
and powerlessness
lives in union with a strange
hope and faith in a Presence
that insists on looking past
my human frailty
and places purpose and destiny
in front of my inability to change.
The greatest gift of God
is love for me despite
my constant turning away.

Wood From The Earth

The wood, from the earth, from creation.
Once a living, growing tree.
Sheltering life. Providing protection. Beautiful.
Made by man into a tool for death.
Carrying the cross.
The weight too much to bear.
It has to be this way.
It has to be this way.
The breaking of body and self will.
It is the journey to freedom from self.
Breaking the chains of control.
Building the power of trust.
Nails, hammer.
Violence.
Weakness? No.
Eye for an eye? No.
Angels rescue? No.
Fathers rescue? No.
Someone help me.
The suffering and pain, when will it stop?
How long can I bear the violence?
Hurtful words.
Abandonment.
I did this for them. Do they know? Will they know?
My courage, my bravery, my love. Will they see?
Will anyone realize?
Am I a failure?
Where is my glory?
Oh, my mother, her pain,
her complete acceptance of the will of my Father.
The spear, it cuts, it pierces through.
My blood, it spills out.
I am following the way and they attack me.
I am offering all of me and they mock and attack me.

Why do they still attack me?
Those who once hailed me now attack me.
Father, forgive them.
My breath is hard, heavy.
The weight of sacrifice is heavy.
Violence laughs. Bitter wine.
All to show them the way.
Can they see it? Are they still blind?
Will they understand my message?
Will they accept it?
Will they be able to follow me?
Will they follow me through the
doorway of the cross?
Will they also be attacked?
I will help them.
I will always be there.
Will they recognize me?
Violence sneers. Where are my disciples?
My arms are wide open.
Will they understand the meaning?
I am completely vulnerable.
I've surrendered control.
I've surrendered all control to my Father.
Father, I give it all to You.
Father, I am in Your Hands.
Will they do this in memory of me?
Will they join me?
Do they understand love?
They will be hurt. They will need to forgive.
They will need to let go.
Will they be my peaceful army?
Will they be set free?

Follow me.

Let go.

Follow me.

Trust me.

It is done.
Violence is defeated.
Forgiveness is triumphant.
Transformation. Resurrection.
Mercy endures from age to age.
Love reigns forever.
Follow me. The Kingdom is at hand.
Open your heart.
Join with me.
Come as you are. Come follow me.
Come into love and live.

Trust Me

Trust me.
I Am always acting in creation.
I Am always acting through you, with you, in you.
The ego stands in the way.
Reject your ego, accept me.
Allow me.
Trust me.

Trust me.
Trust in my Spirit dwelling in you, with you.
For you will be strong, through me.
You will be loving, through me.
You will be merciful, through me.
Have courage, for I am with you always.
Trust me.

Trust me.
Give up your ego, your "self".
Keep simple, keep silent, be joyful for I am with you always,
I bring good even from suffering. This is transformation.
What you give up, I will give back. What you lose, I will
replace. What you need, I will supply. Do this with trust and
complete joy, for I am with you always.
Trust me.

Trust me.
Do not worry.
Do not be afraid.
Smile, for I will never leave you.
Let go. Live free. Trust me.

New Sight

A new journey.

Depression knocks. Sadness shows its face.

Thoughts of aging, pains, worries, time running short.

Wait. Be still. Something is different.

Something has changed.

Love is here. The Spirit is here.

This has never happened before.

It's okay.

It's okay.

Fear is gone.

I've received a gift, a blessing.

It's okay.

Let go, let go, the Spirit is with me.

It's okay.

Come With Me

Come with me on this new journey I've discovered.
I've discovered a flow inside and outside of me.
I've discovered a gift that has always been there.
Come with me on this new journey of joy.

Lift up your head and your heart.
Stand up and then fall deeply into joy and love.
Let go of the false chains that have bound you.
Come with me on this new journey of joy.

Give up the journey you've been following,
full of misguided paths and false judgments.
It's time for a new way, a loving way.
Come with me on this new journey of joy.

Release yourself from your old worn out ways.
Rise up, let go, sing out, feel peace.
You are free to love and to be loved.
You are ready, God is waiting to love you.

Let go of your old self, let go of your old ego.
Empty yourself of yourself.
Become the new person God wants you to be.
Allow yourself to live in God's love.

Come with me and meet the God of all being.
Come with me and meet the God of all creation.
Come with me and meet the God of loving action.
Come with me on this new journey of joy.

Come meet the One who desires your acceptance.
Come meet the One waiting with open arms.
Come meet the One who gives all for you.
Come with me on this new journey of joy.

I Am With You

I am with you in the warmth of the sun.
I am with you in the gentle breeze.
I am with you in the living soil.
I am with you in the life-giving waters.

I am with you when life seems abundant.
I am with you when the bottom seems near.
I am with you when you feel I've left you.
I am with you when you turn me away.

I am with you in the friendly smile.
I am with you in the gentle embrace.
I am with you in the kind blessings.
I am with you in the simple hello.

I am with you in your suffering and pain.
I am with you in your loneliness and sorrow.
I am with you in sadness and emptiness.
You are not alone, you are never alone.

I am with you in all of creation.
I am with you from beginning to end.
I am with you in the transformation.
Infinite, Incarnate, Intimate.

I am with you in the storm.
I am with you in the silence.
Inside you, outside you, all around you.
Rest in my presence, I am here.

Immersed

We are immersed in creation,
therefore, we are immersed in Christ.
Christ is the joining of spirit and matter,
incarnate, in all creation.

The light that I see.
The air that I breathe.
The ground that I touch.
The sounds that I hear.
The food that I taste.
All experiences with Christ.

We are never separate from Christ, or we would die.
Even then, we are not separate but transformed in Christ.

Creation is a blessing.
Bless the sun, which provides warmth and light.
Bless the wind, which provides life-giving breath.
Bless be the wind which brings scent to our nose.
Bless the wind, which carries sound to our ears.
Bless the earth, which provides endless ways
to touch and to be touched.
Bless the earth, which provides food for our sustenance.
Bless all creation.
May we reverence and respect all creation as a
gift of Christ.

Beings Of Matter And Light

We are beings of matter and light.
We live in that thin membrane,
that fine web between matter and light.
We live in that tension between
the physical world and the spiritual world.

In this state of tension,
we are pulled upon by compassion and violence.
We remain connected to both,
but we are given the grace of freedom.
We have the freedom to allow compassion
or violence to flow, pulling the balance toward
one or the other, living with a greater sense
of peace or fear.

The longer we spend toward one or the other
slowly provides our transformation.
The more we allow flow toward love,
the closer we move toward the source of love,
and the more we become united with the All.

Freedom

I've been given the gift of spiritual freedom.
I've been set free from the need for knowledge of spiritual
things but instead gained the need for a full heart.
I've been set free from theology and dogma.
I've been set free of my need to control everything.
I've been set free from my ego,
my need to impress, to explain.

I've been set free of the need to explain but instead gained the
desire to offer simple acts of love.
I've been set free from fear and guilt but instead gained the
desire to receive and offer compassion.
I've been set free to become empty, in order that I may be
filled with peace and contentment.
I've been set free to allow love to flow through me, allowing
myself to be a vessel to connect with others.
I've been set free to comfort, listen, and love, without saying a
word, nor comment, nor theory.
I've been set free to appreciate and love all of creation.
I've been set free from the past and the future, receiving the
gift of the present, the moment, the immediate.

I've been given the gift to allow myself to be loved, nurtured
and forgiven in every moment of every day.
I've been set free from the power of death and have been
given the gift of transformation, of resurrection, of union with
the everlasting source of All.
Can you think of a greater gift of grace and blessing?
Breathe in, breathe out.
Give thanks and praise, love endures forever.

Purify

What will be left when this purification ends,
when the meat is carved from the bones?
I fall into a depression.
This is surely not my will.

You are here.

It is true that when we die, we die alone.
Even spiritual death is not exempt from this truth.
I did not expect this, where is joy?
I did not see my resistance, my pride.

You are here.

What is it that you want from me?
What path are you placing before me?
What is it that I should do?
This is not how I thought it would be.

I will continue to trust you.

Yes, I will trust you.
Yes, I will trust you.
Yes, I do love you.
Yes, I will surrender to you.

There are certainly those who suffer greater than I.
Each soul has their own dark night.
But you have not left me alone.
You are not gone, you have not abandoned me.

You are here, I am not lost.

This path, this spiritual walk along to Empty,
is filled with the stripping of all held dear.
Understanding that my struggle is coming,
I am to march on, even embracing the holy struggle.

This hidden purification, my personal journey,
is an internal struggle, a raging battle of wills.

The Spirit Moves Me

The Spirit moves me.
A slow burning inside.
I realize my human weakness.
Through warm tears and hopeful heart, I come in petition.
Grasping for healing or mercy or guidance, I groan for help.
I am still.

The Spirit moves me.
There are moments.
There is light, there is joy.
In these times I recognize blessings.
Humbled, grateful, I race in front
of my ego far enough to give thanks.
I am still.

The Spirit moves me.
I begin to search.
Stumbling like a newborn's first steps.
Stepping, doubting, falling.
Confused about why this urge began,
Why am I different?
I am still.

The Spirit moves me.
I continue to search.
Wrong place, right place.
I am blind, why can't I see?
I try so hard but darkness remains.
Why can't I see?
I am still.

The Spirit moves me.
Humility. Ego. Pride.
I will move to empty.
The struggle will be constant
and the process will be slow.
I am still.

The Spirit moves me.
Many paths, many journeys.
Life and death intertwined.
Faith vanishes but hope remains.
Plans and ambitions are like clouds,
both easily blown away with the wind.
I am still.

I am aware.
I acknowledge that I am small.
I acknowledge the deep.
I am humble and simply acknowledge that I cannot fully
know the deep.
Only the deep can make itself known as the Spirit wills.
I wait. I prepare an open heart.
I am still.

Chapter 3   Into The Deep

Time and before time.
Incarnate and before incarnation.
Energy and life.

Human-ness

Participate with the greatness of creation.
Participate with the mystical
providence of being human.
This gift of the Creator, being human,
has for too long been considered dirty,
sinful, flawed, something to be shed
like a useless worn out garment.
When, in fact, this gift is the chosen
reality for our journey to a reunion with the First.
This gift is so special and integral to reality
that the Creator is physically present and woven
through, with, in our very human experience
in the first incarnation (the big bang).
This was the plan from the beginning.
We are not meant to deny our humanity
but to allow it to bring us to fulfillment.

Love, human-ness, forgiveness,
faith, hope, life are all bonded together
in our journey in a beautiful display
of the Divine imprint in all creation.

Ego

Sometimes I have to remember not to be too hard on my Ego. It's like a little child wanting to impress and to be special.

It makes me laugh.

I have to laugh at myself, my ego, and the silly things that pop into my mind about how I could be important or noticed. My Ego is quite good at this, running short movies in my head of what I could do and what others would then think about me.

Well, I am important, but not because of what I do or say, but because I'm loved.

Humanity

This life.
Real.
Dynamic.
Filled with living relationships.
Good ones. Bad ones.
Tough, gritty, dirty.
Loving, laughing, kicking, screaming, crying.
Hurting, losing, dying.

Each day we get a new chance to get up,
stand, fall, kneel, crawl, fall again.
It's not hard to lose sight of the holy,
the beautiful, the mystery,
as we struggle through the everyday
journey of our life.

Struggles. Suffering.
Not obstacles to being holy.
Our direct path to being holy.
Real human struggles.
Real human relationships.
Holy opportunities.
Opportunities to love.
They are hard.
Sometimes they hurt.
We fail.
We suffer.
We cry.
We groan.
We let go.
We wait.
We hope.
We trust.

We transform.
We become selfless.
We accept forgiveness.
We forgive.
We heal.
The beauty of Human.

Peace and struggle
are bound together.
Joy and sacrifice.
Divinity and humanity.
Creator and created.

Even during periods of spiritual growth, suffering still presides. Notice, however, that our response changes. We still suffer, but we notice God's presence during our suffering. We notice the presence of the Spirit carrying us through our transformation. This is an incredible change when we realize we're not alone, but we are greatly cherished.

Human Struggle - A Cry for Help

The knives and arrows continue to come,
hitting my body with precision,
slowly breaking down this living vessel.
The damage occurs and the wounds are deep.
I don't even know why I'm in this fight.
It's choosing me, I don't want it.
I reach out for support, there's no one there.
I cry out for help but I am alone.
My chest is tight, my anxiety is high.
Yet I can still see light.
I do not understand. My mind swirls.
I feel sick, I want to hide. I want to scream.
My body hurts and is wounded.

But You are here, I can feel Your presence.
I do not carry this burden alone.
From the middle of my struggle, You give peace.
From the intensity of my battle,
I'm looking for rage and release through anger,
You give me calm.

I am about to break, I am close to drowning,
but You grab my hand.
You pull me up and lift me out of danger.
Even as the enemy destroys my body
You embrace my soul and Spirit.

I cannot explain this. It does not fit with my human will. It flows against the stream. Pry open this box of suffering that I so carefully protect. I feel off balance. Among the stress and anxiety, my spirit is still. While my body aches, my soul is quiet. It is like leading a double life, but no, spirit and body are connected. I stop, slowly notice, and a subtle smile arises from the gift I'm being given. How can this be? Even within the pain, You are here. You are with me in my suffering. You are teaching me the way. You are guiding me through my transformation, refining me with fire.

The Human Spirit

The human spirit is very beautiful,
even when one is suffering or in pain.
The beauty of the life, the fight, the desire for peace,
the surrounding loved ones provides an amazing
story of creation, life, and yes, of transformation.
These beautiful spirits are examples,
they are teachers, they are trailblazers, they are to be
cherished and held in great esteem.
They are bearers of deep spiritual meaning.
They are diamonds, the results of great refinement.
And mostly, they are our closest connection
to life and love and transformation.
Rest assured that the Holy Spirit is very close to these spirits,
guiding them on their eternal journey.

Be awake, be aware of these special spirits.
Take notice of these moments,
these glimpses into a soul that is treasured by the One.

Every part of creation writes a story.
Each human spirit creates a poem of life.
Allow yourself to read them,
to immerse yourself into them, to be open to them.

Breath

Breath.
Spirit. Life.
Union. One.
An offering of self.
An opening of self.
Joining deep with deep.

I have at times brushed past
the moment of dying to self.
I have felt it. I have thought about it.
I have touched it.

I have contemplated it.
But, I have not become it.
I have not made it my own.

An offering of self.
An opening of self.
Joining deep with deep.
Selflessness,
like compassion,
is a decision.

Big Bang. Perhaps the big bang was an explosion of Love, reaching out, expanding in an outward act of creation. At some point all will rejoin with the One, the Source of this loving explosion, to become once again united, transformed and in never-ending beauty.

Creation

Creation is a resurrection.
All creation is constantly going through resurrection.
As science shows all things go through change and can transform into something else.
Resurrection is part of our transformation.
Death is part of our resurrection.
Love is continuously transforming.
Suffering is part of our transformation.
Pain is part of our transformation,
providing memory/value of this process,
no matter what rules or religions we may have created.
We are not separated from each other,
only by our own false distinctions.
What is truth? Love is truth.

Our whole purpose is transformation and resurrection.
Our whole purpose is a journey of total
reconnection to the Creator.
We have freedom. We have the freedom to accept or reject.
Any rejection is something we create within our freedom.
True love is never forced.
Our journey is to fulfill Love's energy through us.
This is becoming that for which we were created.

The Language Of The Spirit Is Love

The language of the Spirit is Love.
The language of the Spirit is awareness.
The language of the Spirit is connectedness.
This language is spoken in our hearts,
our soul, our being.

We must keep ourselves open to hear the Spirit.
We must keep quiet, vocally and spiritually.
We must be aware, listening with an heart open.

Connectedness.
Joining.
Joining with the Truth.
Joining physically and spiritually.
Connected through love.
All is gift, all is grace, all is love.
This gift is not earned, but only received,
accepted or refused.

We were created to allow
the expression of love,
the flowing of love,
the ultimate act of love,
the re-joining.

The Encounter

God reaches forth...

With indescribable humility, we accept.

This reality, this moment, or many such moments, is the defining action of our entire purpose. All else falls away or becomes secondary to this action of relationship, of union, of love.

This comes in the most tender of moments, the purest, the most innocent. Free from all self, ego, external source. This is where our true identity, our true spirit, in the stillness of time, eyes cast downward in glorious humility, is grateful that this offer remains. We reach back...

and accept the love of God.

This is the beginning of existence in union.

The Vale

Ultimately, the vale between the spirit and the body is very thin, if it even exists at all. If there is a boundary, then it is likely one we have created ourselves or as part of our created being with the idea that with transformation the spirit and body will be more intensely joined. This can be seen in the life story of Jesus.

This Spirit of creation is in everyone and all created things, shining with brilliance and beauty for those with eyes of love to see. The ability to see in this way is extremely transformational to our own being, changing everything about how we view and experience the world around us, but especially how we see (and relate to) our brothers and sisters. We are truly learning to see with the eyes of Christ. This is incredible Grace at work.

Nameless

This unity.
This relationship.
Nameless.
No words. None needed.
Emptiness and fullness.
Not mine, but my true being.
Presence in all presence.
Presence inside and outside.
Presence in the world and outside the world.
Presence in Christ.
Receiving the moment with confidence and joy.
"Free to go in and out of infinity".

(Quote attributed to Thomas Merton)

Completed

Spirituality is not sharp.
It's not full of rough edges
but it's a smooth flow towards Union.
It's not full of hard rules and sharp demands
that we have to do or not do,
but smooth like a wave.
Creation is good.
We are precious to God,
who loves us beyond
our understanding.
Although we are incomplete in this life
it is through God that we will be made whole
and brought to full Union.
Life is a smooth wave
as we experience ups and downs
in our move towards Union.

Spirit Of Life (Next Journey Explained)

A friend of mine recently died, and as I contemplated my friends being, I could see a shape, a fluidly moving shape, surrounded by a boundary of light, hovering with a little hesitation before another presence. I'm sure this was in my imagination, but it seemed pleasant. This is when I was inspired to write the following poem.

The Next Journey

Shhhh....be quiet.
Be calm...
I am here for you.
I am with you.

You have labored hard.
You have suffered much.
Come, it is over.
Do not be afraid.
Come, it is time to rest.

Come.
Come into my light.
Do not be afraid.
You are like a star of light.
With complete openness,
allow your light to join my eternal light.
Be joined with the source of all light.
Be joined with inexpressible love.

Let your spirit rejoice.
Come, fall into my love.
Do not be afraid.
Fall into everlasting joy.
Fall into everlasting peace.

You have been made new.
You are spirit, you are free.
Come take your place in
my heavenly kingdom.

Feel my embrace.
You are loved,
oh how greatly you are loved.
You are home.
Welcome home.
Peace forever.

(Dedicated to my friend Alice)

Floating

We are floating in the Spirit/Presence/Being of God (a good description of the Trinity, right). There really isn't a here or there, or God is here and we are there. There really isn't Time. There really isn't this place or that place. There is only the presence of God. We are floating in the being of God with a thin veil called death between the physical world and Spirit world. There really is no Time after death (or before birth). Time is only a feature of the physical world.

Death is just a doorway or passageway which transforms us from physical body and Spirit to spirit body and Spirit. Death is a tunnel that we pass through in which we shed our physical body and rise and are resurrected into our new spirit body.

In this transformation of death, our physical ego-self is stripped away and no longer exists and the state of our real self is revealed. The state of our real self is not really based on what we have done or didn't do. This is false Theology because we cannot earn our union with God. This state of being is based on how we allowed ourselves to be consumed by God's love.

The Mirror

A mirror does not feel or seek fulfillment.
A mirror simply, humbly reflects.
It does not receive an image and
hold onto it trying to gain something for itself.
As quickly as the image comes, reflection takes place.
The mirror does not try to take credit for the reflection.
It does not own the thing being reflected.
It does not own anything other than its presence
inside of the great presence.
If it has peace it's in the simple fact of allowing
its purpose to be achieved, of being its purpose,
of being what it was created to be.
Being anything else causes tension and friction with reality.
A mirror does not spend time trying to be a hat stand.
Nor does it find anything to boast about it being a mirror.

This mirror that I speak of is the mirror of your heart and soul
and is a special and unique mirror.
It is not a judging mirror.
It is a searching mirror.
This mirror searches in all things for the image of God.
It looks far and wide and deep for this image,
and finds its true purpose in reflecting this image of Love.

Chapter 4 Prayer

Contemplation

Contemplation allows me
to travel to another place,
a place of presence,
for I do not visit this place often.
It allows me to empty myself.
It allows me to listen,
to listen with my heart.

The New Place

Not knowing...
Just letting...
Just allowing...
In a state of wonder...

Here, questions and answers are the same things.
Here, questions and answers slowly drift away
in a sea of unknowing, carried away in the winds
of acceptance, losing any importance
in the presence of Love.
Here, we're nothing when we follow our own will.
Here our will is empty and useless.
We present ourselves without reserve
to the unexplainable mystery.

Here there are no words.
There is no way to describe the mystery.
We relinquish our need for meaning,
pure contentment needs no purpose.

Just waiting in awe...
Giving all of the self to the
reality beyond our understanding,
in quiet wonder of this mystery.

Early Stages Meditation

Trying to visualize the point in my center, that point which is deeper than my thoughts which swirl around in commotion. Deeper than my emotions which are a sea of unpredictable feelings. Deeper than my ego and it's self-absorbed ideas of who or what I think I should be. I visualize a point that represents my beginning when my being was whispered into existence. A point created with intention of life and beauty. A point beyond my reach, beyond my first awareness of self, beyond my control. I visualize a small but very intense, swirling ball of light, a circular form of life-giving energy. In this center, I have no thoughts, words, actions. If thoughts come, I've left the center. In this place, I'm only openness, patience, humility, awareness. This is the place of waiting. This is the place of timelessness and unknowing.

All I can do here is wait, eyes lowered, hands folded and knees bent, in silence.
I wait...
I listen...
I become not I...
I become true self...
I wait…

This place is a place of purity, not blemished by my thoughts, words, actions. This is why I imagined it as white light, as a white room. I saw my parents faces and was reminded of my pure beginning, the moment before my self-ego began. This is the holy place that is connected to all things, not a separate or secluded place. This is why I still saw my bodily self in this room. I am not separated from the world in this place, but this is where my true self can emanate to reach out to the world from humble purity.

Meditation 2

The following is just a worded description of what I am experiencing in my journey into meditation. It's not meant to be a statement of Faith, only a description from my point of view.

Today I visualized the point at my center. I visualized a small but very intense, swirling ball of light, a circular form of life-giving energy.
I moved close to this light, trying to enter into this place. Initially, it seemed like I could simply place my head into this space. It was what seemed like a room, a pure white room, completely empty and without definable walls. Each time my mind tried to label or define, my head came out of the room. As I put my head back into the room, I attempted to be blank, to just be present. I could hold this for a while, but then my mind would engage in trying to identify. Slowly it seemed like I was able to enter the room. It was pure white. I decided to follow my own poetic advice and just wait, just be present with no expectations or self-will. Eventually, I became aware that this is not an out of body experience, but that while in this contemplative state, I'm still very much connected with the physical world. I could still hear noises, I could still feel my knees hurting from kneeling. I could still concentrate on my breathing. I could now sense that I was kneeling in the white room. I was kneeling at a white altar rail.
I continued to wait.

At one point I saw the face of my mother, then of my mother and father together. I felt happy. I tried not to latch on to this or to understand.
I continued to wait.

The time was over for this session of meditation, time to return to work. As I left the church and walked outside, I had a moment where my senses seemed heightened. Things looked brighter, more vibrant. It would've been nice to sit and meditate at this moment.

Meditation 3 (What is real)

What's real is real, but not for the reason we think.

We are created with both an outer life and an interior life. The outer and interior life are intrinsically connected. We mostly see through the perspective of our outer life. The interior life perspective can only be seen when we have emptied ourselves of our ego and selfishness. Our inner life only seems empty because we are so accustomed to seeing things from the perspective of our outer life. But in fact, the inner life can be very rich and full, filled with the presence of Christ, of love, of life and creation if we but allow it. This inner "center place" of meditation is not a small place, in fact, it is not a place at all but an endlessly infinite expanse within God. We can only be present to it, glimpse it, draw strength from it, find peace in it, fall in love with it. We cannot know or understand or comprehend this place, just as we cannot understand or comprehend God. We just know this interior place is free of self, it lives under the cover of our outer selves, it is deep and unaffected by our ego and the outer life. This is the place where the Spirit resides. This is the place of pure intention.

The interior life directly affects the outer life. It reaches out and longs for and connects to the center in all things, the "true" purpose in things, the "true" being especially in our brothers and sisters. This is deep calling to deep.

In The Stillness

Be still.
Wait with Me.
Listen.
Be present.
Be with me, I Am here.

Beyond words.
Beyond understanding.
Beyond explanations.
Be present with Me.
Let go of your will.

Be silent.
Wait with Me,
without your words,
without your thoughts,
without your way.

Be still.
Wait with Me.
Feel My Presence.
Accept My Presence.
Be with Me, I Am here.

Quiet.
I Am before your words.
I Am before your thoughts or plans.
Wait with Me.
I Am here.

Chapter 5

Journey to the Heart

Year Of The Heart

I am now entering the year of the heart.
The time for words is coming to a close.

I am loved by my beloved,
and I choose to wear this love
like a garment of light,
moving through this world offering hope,
searching for the true nature of love in everyone
I meet and in the created world around me.

I must broaden my view.
I need to to see through eyes of love,
seeing the whole versus only the parts.
I have been given a message,
now I need to turn and share with others.

I am to be a carrier of souls.
I am to be a guide, to shine light on beginning,
middle, and end, to be a provider of hope
in a world that is crying out for God.

Awake

Be awake.

Be aware.

Take notice.

God is always present, waiting to meet you,
waiting to dance.

Immerse yourself in the moment,
in the presence of all Creation.
Immerse yourself warmly in relationships,
seeking out the presence of the inner beauty
of each true being,
gladly finding the life giving presence.

Engage with others, engage with the whole person.
Try to engage at the "heart level".
Be open to your heart to guide you in this work.
Live life robustly with great joy.
Be awake. Be aware. Take notice.

New Day Observations

Simple observations,
the sun's life giving ray's warming our skin,
beautiful trees providing the air for our
breathing in and breathing out,
a bright clear sky providing our protection
from the harshness of space.

The new day provides chances to experience
connectedness and enjoying the sacredness of life,
joining in the playful dance of the Creator with creation,
gaining the joy of heart from glimpses
of boundless expressions of love.

Imagine

Imagine the beautiful glory of a small child gleefully noticing a butterfly sitting in the bushes while playing on a sunny warm day. Then, the child is filled with wonder as it takes flight displaying it's magical movements and vibrant colors.

This is the same kind of wonder felt when one discovers the grace filled gift of love offered by the Creator for no apparent reason other than delight in us. We haven't earned it. We haven't reasoned it. It's a simple childlike discovery of a treasure found inexplicably among all the other distractions we thought were critical to our destiny. It comes at that moment when it's least expected. It may come in a moment of great need, or in a simple quiet moment of contemplation and introspection. We immediately smile in joy at the simple directness of this gift, knowing it's beyond our understanding and ability to bring forth ourselves. Yes, we are truly and greatly loved beyond our imagination, no matter what.

I'm truly thankful and in love with the One who bestows such gifts of unexplainable love upon me, and will continue to be in wonder at the outpouring and reception of this Great Love.

Heart Silence

In the silence.
No words are spoken.
No words needed.
No words will do.

Heart to heart.
Relationship.
Love feelings.
Explanations fall short.

Possible.
Not possible.
This matters not.
All gift, all grace.

I want to share.
No words are available.
Logical mind?
The mind is silent.

Let go of pride.
Let go of control,
lofty doctrine or creed.
Lost in grace alone.

Struggle free, cross free?
Suffering remains.
But wait, this love
sustains even in pain.

How can this be?
No logic, no reason.
Happiness, quick smile,
unexpected peace.

Glimpses.
Moments.
Unthinkable.
No words are possible.

Lonely? Maybe in
the human sense.
Solitude. Inner life.
Deep unto deep.

Born

I was born again this morning,
in a simple, quiet way.
Any time I realize that my path
has nothing to do with what I want,
with my plans, my ways,
I am born again in the Spirit
and given new life.

Mystery

Mystery solved with mystery.
The unexplainable blown away
in the wisdom of spiritual wonder.
A castaway in life's journey toward light.

My journey has never really been to a place.
Rather, it is a journey to the heart,
to a state of pure presence,
the unknown place I have always been.

What then of the demand for answers
and the unending quest to own truth?
Turns out to not be a quest at all,
for this truth cannot be contained by man.

The heart accepts mystery as it is.
The heart embraces the unknown.
Here the unknown is not a threat,
humanness joining with divine.

You Know

You know Me.
You know Me.
You know Me.

Heart, not mind.
Love, not thought.
Compassion, not proclamation.

In tears of pain.
In tears of joy.
Deep unto deep.

Contemplation of heart.
Presence of heart.
Feel. You do know Me.

Lord, why do you love me?
I love you because you are you.
I love you as I made you.

I love you and I need you.
Here I am Lord.
What shall I do?

I Am Present.
Be with Me.
Love Me.

Give praise, give praise.
For in great compassion,
love is made known.

An explosion of the cosmos.
Baby in a manger.
Glory comes.

Incarnation.
Reincarnation.
Circle of love.

Life.
Love.
Union.

Christmas Message

Awestruck by the graces given.
Embraced with ancient energy,
images of eternal love granted.
Heaven telling the glory of God,
all creation shouting with joy.

A star brings forth the moment,
we are immersed in
the reality of the Love God.
Heavens first kiss longing
for union with its beloved.

Love incarnate, first woven into
our life through the fabric of creation.
Christ through mother and Spirit,
Alpha and Omega made known,
Gift of eternal union, a baby is born.

Joined for all eternity in a bond
of physical and spiritual communion.
Loving hand of the Father reaching
forth in the vulnerable innocence of
pure and complete selfless love.

Search no longer, God is near.
In the stillness, the gentle whisper
carrying your heart to the place
of mystery, both infinite and intimate,
knowable only through love pangs.

Stand firm in the beacon light
of hope dear cosmic travelers.
The One Love has blessed you,
now daughters and sons of truth,
children of Eternal Light and Love.

Let Heaven and Earth rejoice.
God became human so we
can become one with God.
Let the merry banquet begin.
Loving union offered to all.

Relationship

Conscious decision?
Perhaps a simple acceptance of
this ever present love affair.
Where my human mind lacks focus,
my heart was made for communion.

All relationship is with God, since all being
is through this same connection.
Life in Christ, Christ in life.
Simply open your heart and allow
true living and being to flourish.

Single Drop

I am but a single drop of water in a moving river, carried by the power and flow, rushing into the waiting sea which is the Infinite One Source.

How can I be thankful enough for the divine river flow other than simply letting it carry me freely into the unknown, allowing myself to be carried into wholeness, becoming one with the flowing waters of life.

Sanctuary

I sacrifice my knowledge-ego
to obtain the grace of heart peace.
In the sanctuary shadows my
prayers rise like mystic incense.

In the sanctuary heaven born
whispers reach through the
unseen vale stealing deep
groans of love echoes.

I become still, and quietly listen.
I smile, because I know you're here.
I am a child, brother, heir to a great fortune.
Treasured soulmate, Kingdom come.

Everything

Everything flows.
Everything moves in
union with the divine flow.
The Universe visits through
the infinite breath of life.

The Universal Prayer
is ever changing Creation.
Everything transforms in
life changing motion.
Attachment begets death.

The inner mirror provides
transforming glimpses
of the truth of eternity.
Gift, blessing, life,
giving rest in peaceful hope.

Infinite expressions of
relation-building presence
carrying all creation toward
oneness and joyful union.
We remain open to the mystery.

Chapel Simplicity

I am still, I am quiet.
God is Love in the quiet.
God is Love in my breath,
breathe in slowly,
breathe out in peace.

I am still, I am quiet.
God is love in the flicker
of sunlight flashing
playfully on the chapel wall.
Breathe in, breathe out.

God is love in the friendly
smile of the silent fellow
disciple who arrived with hope
filled eyes and open heart.
We sit quietly, heart speak.

God is in the heartbeats,
silent mantras of both
joys and sorrows cascading
forth in a passion flow.
Breathe in, breathe out.

God is love in the tears,
memories of loved ones.
If stories were told they
would be divinely infused
raw emotions of life.

I am still, I am quiet.
God is in my humility,
my recognition of my
unknowing, my blindness.
My inner child rejoices.

Breathe in, breathe out.
Breathe in, breathe out.
The cadence clears my mind.
Breathe in slowly,
breathe out in peace.

Room of silence, so quiet
my heart rhythm provides
ancient music from my spirit
born earthen vessel, waiting
in love's soft contentment.

Your Name (night)

Lord, this life burns out before
You on the altar of days.
May Your Name be praised.
May Your Name be praised.

Lord, in the night I am quiet,
reflecting on the true nature,
reflecting on the follies of men.
May Your Holy Name be praised.

Lord, You are with me in the deep night.
Teach me to embrace the silence,
teach me to accept a heart of mercy.
May Your Holy Name be praised.

Lord, let my joys and sorrows
burn like incense before You.
In my silence, my soul rests in You.
Father, Son, and Spirit be praised.

Being

I am quiet.
Being.
No thoughts of religion,
good or bad.

I am present.
Being.
No planning,
no comparing.

Being.
You are here.
I am present in You.
I am free.

I am present.
You are here.
Everything open.
Creation at play.

Being.
Open forgiveness.
No offense carried.
Cling to no grievance.

I am with You.
Kingdom come,
even if a glimpse,
like Heaven on Earth.

I am present.
Ego self becomes
know in the presence
of Light, of Truth.

Light and Truth
sheds our ego self.
Our true being now
free to rest in love.

Being.
Deeper than self.
True being lives
here with You.

When I repent,
yes, when I turn
toward Your face,
love is always there.

Being.
Spirit moving where
it wills filling hearts
with contentment.

I am present.
Here I am Yours.
Nothing else matters,
loved beyond words.

I am quiet,
I cannot explain.
Who would believe
if not experienced?

Being, this place.
I want to share.
Unexplainable,
words cannot begin.

Being, in this place
I want to lead.
Get away pride,
God's ways unknown.

I am quiet.
The Reign will share.
The Reign will lead.
Kingdom come.

Being.
Great treasures in
the Kingdom Reign.
Compassion and mercy.

Incarnation.
One love, one source
laid open and for all,
from age to age.

Beginning presence.
Presence now.
Presence forever.
Amen Amen.

My Life

I am in the universe,
and the universe is in the One.
My breath is in the One.
My life is in the One.
Blessings and peace abound.

Praise Christ!
For this we were created,
Light shining it's
rays of fulfilling love
into my awaiting heart.

Praise the Holy Spirit,
the life giving force
that travels through me
and in me causing my
heart to burn with desire.

My spirit rejoices in
peace and contentment,
like a small child swept
up in the loving arms of his
doting and protective mother.

Praise the blessed freedom
received in the forgiveness
of my weaknesses.
I embrace this gift of Grace
with head bowed in humility.

In this Kingdom my being
dances with joy, joining
in the great dance inside
the wonders of creation.
Praise Christ the Incarnate.

Real

Real.
Real-ness.
Reality.
Presence in the present.

Openness.
Awareness.
Awake.
Awake to what is real.

Eyes open.
Aware of surroundings.
No reviewing or planning.
Simply breathing, living.

Here I am.
I am here to be with You.
I am here.
You are here.

Life is real.
I am living.
Moments.
Dynamic moments.

Expression of Creation.
Incarnation expression.
Life expression.
Relationship expression.

Boundless expression.
Everlasting.
Expression through us
and in us. We are expression.

Once an expression becomes incarnate, it is everlasting. Expressions are dynamic, constantly transforming, but always real and present. What has been created cannot be destroyed. This is why we believe in Eternity. Creation evolves through relationship and transformation. This relationship is opening, emptying, giving, receiving. As you can see by its nature it is dynamic and transformational.

Look

Look, look.
Open your eyes and see.
See the truth in the present
reality displayed before you.

Awaken from your false dream.
You search here and there like
an unsure, confused student,
face downward reading words.

How is it that when looking
for the Creator of all things
you do not actually look at
the wonders of Creation?

We are created in the likeness
and image of our Creator.
We live in and move and have
our being, offsprings of the First.

Life is not out there.
Truth and Love are not out there,
but are like the wind,
blowing in and through all,
sustaining all in Light.

We are connected through the visible
and invisible life blood which
continuously pours forth from
the relational expression of Creation.

Open

I am here to be with You.
I am open to You.
I acknowledge Your Presence.
I am open to Reality.

My being is an expression
of reality. You are Reality.

Living in the present,
free from preconceptions,
each moment a new surprise,
each moment a new blessing.

This relationship of existence,
with each new moment,
is God's powerful incarnate
display of loving Grace.

God opens to allow
our freedom reflection,
our yes-no acceptance
of the Love-God's Self.

Invisible God? Silent God?
Everyone open your eyes,
everyone open your hearts,
reality bursting forth everywhere.

See God, be with God.
Embrace each moment
of the act of Creation.
Engage body, spirit, soul.

God of moments,
God of ever blessed moments,
each moment filled with the
quiet ecstasy of Pure Love.

For now I can only see glimpses,
flashes of Eden memories,
what was, what is, what will be fused
in the timelessness of Real Presence.

The Healing

Fifty years long
I have been blind,
a few times Insight
sharing small truths.

Eyes now opened,
light pouring into
a soul hungry and
thirsty for sustenance.

This new food is
sweeter than honey,
satisfying a craving,
a longing for Wisdom.

Like a young child
I cautiously move
toward this teacher, eyes
open wide and hopeful.

Is there danger?
Trust in Love.
If it is truth,
truth always.

Am I ready?
Will my response
be one of openness,
allowance, acceptance?

I've been blind
for so long.
Old methods,
habits and ways.

I've been blind
for so long.
Clouds leave long
dark shadows.

Trust in Me.
Way.
Truth.
Life.

Truth comes in heart
pangs, love callings,
not explanations.
Kingdom humility.

Truth comes in emptiness,
unknowing, selflessness.
Let the children come,
The Kingdom of God is theirs.

My move to empty
has finally lead to
a heart opening.
True, real, surprising.

Chapter 6
In Need of Grace

Even in the Light, there will be times when we struggle with the darkness

Test

The test has come again.
The test of faith,
the test of spirit,
the test always comes.

A significant strike,
in the guise of academia,
in the mask of confidence,
logic and dissuasion.

This attack came not of the heart,
but directed straight at the ego-self,
an offering of earthly knowledge,
pride arriving before the fall.

I stumbled.
Doubt struck at my heart.
I fell to the ground,
I fell into darkness.

But this time was different.
I've stumbled before,
I've languished in darkness
and lost the light in my eyes.

This time there was a hand,
this time the light did not leave,
this time my faith was
carried on the wings of Grace.

This strength is not my strength,
this power is not my power.
In my weakness I am held,
in my emptiness I am filled.

What kind of love is this
that reaches down so low
as to rescue the unworthy?
What kind of love is this?

This love is higher than this world.
This mystery is from the I Am.
All I can do is open my heart.
All I can do is accept being saved.

I give thanks for the unknown mystery.
My heart captured by unspeakable peace.
I walk while keeping a humble spirit.
I live within the Light of the world.

Sinners Hope

(Part One)

The test has come.
The test of my darkness,
the test always comes.

Fall, fall again.
I have fallen again
into the darkness.

I have chosen darkness again.
Fucking darkness.
Why do I love darkness?

Burn me.
Burn away my disease.
Burn me.

Transform in fire,
or pain, or whatever
will remove my disgust.

Have I truly gotten nowhere
except for a mouthful of words?
I'm a charlatan of lofty damn words.

Once again, Ego is unmasked.
I've chosen Ego,
my God-damned Ego.

Burn it away.
Free me from this prison.
Free me from this misery.

(Part Two)

The test has come.
The test of my darkness,
the test always comes.

In a world of make believe,
this way, that way, not me.
My heart is bursting at the
thought that this is not me.
The ride of Grace is eclipsed,
the mighty ego world has lifted
it's head and said, "I am here".
The mighty ego world has
pushed it's stone soul, it's black
darkness in front of the Light.
O Lord, I don't know how much
longer I can hold out, I'm tired.
Poker faces and shifting eyes,
ego world's crashing and pushing
and pretending that they are
pursuing the dream, the way.
Crush me with your false promise,
shape me and mold me into your
sycophant drone army of followers.
Yes, yes you have your way,
I'm too weak now to stand strong.

But I warn you now, the Love of the
mighty One has pierced my heart.
I have been given the taste of the
mystical embrace.

So yes, the test has come, and although I am stumbling, and
I'm a bit dazed and confused,
I will keep picking myself up and offering my
open heart, and when I finally gain the courage to love, I will
join Victory in the unveiling of the inseparable union, ego
destroyed forever more.

The Battle

The epic battle of my
Move to Empty is at hand.
Powerful Ego, integrated into
my very being, difficult to dethrone.

I continue to try to impose
expectations on others,
at the same time not seeing
myself clearly in the mirror,
not seeing my own denial of fate.

I fail to recognize the battle,
the fight that I have entered.
I fail to give respect to my struggle,
secretly oppose my transformation,
continue to deny my love-destiny.

The ego's desire to fight
and defend almost unbreakable.
I pray for my transformation everyday.
I ask for my ego to be burned away,
but my courage for the road to Calvary is hollow.

This vision has become clear.
I can no longer deny its Light.
Yes, surprised at the Via Dolorosa.
Is there another way?
Can I survive the weight of this cross.

The vulnerability can be
too much to bear.
The humiliations, scowls,
ridicule and embarrassment
too much to withstand.

To knowingly proceed to ones
crucifixion requires great sacrifice.
The process can be devastating.
For a proud, improvident man
this sacrifice may be impossible.

A choice to make,
to allow events to come forth,
needed for deep transformation.
The strength needed to become
restored to inner sanctity is Divine.

The darkness is coming near.
The truth, this cup cannot pass.
Rebirth through sacrificing self.
Father, thy will is hard.
Let it come, Thy Will be done.

Life Burning

Life burning away,
deeply burning.
What cause deserves
the value of my life?

What is it that
drives my veiled
existence, desiring
these shallow treasures.

No, not shallow,
but also not deep.
What happens now that
I've discovered true deep?

The trenches I've dug
are deep, sure enough.
I follow them like a
proud and loyal soldier.

My life burns like an
offering to a golden calf,
yet sometimes I hear
Truth whisper my name.

Do I recognize Truth?
Dimly, through the haze
of smoldering embers,
my vision briefly clears.

My struggle continues.
How long will I ignore
the message of my heart,
trapped in my own prison?

Chapter 7
Move To Love

*"Just a simple man, on a simple journey
with an amazing God"*

Wisdom

Like a cool morning breeze,
Wisdom is blowing over me,
speaking with my soul,
pronouncing Real Presence
in the language of the Spirit.

Joy of joys,
moving as you will through
the open spaces of my heart.
I am filled with contentment,
my being caught in the moment,
a world between heaven and Earth.

Giving thanks.
Giving praise.
Precious moments are woven
in the fabric of time.

Golden Cathedral

Golden Cathedral,
a chapel window into
life. My heart longs to
overflow with this Grace.

Silently awaiting the
unseen spiritual wonder.
Real Presence cloaked
in simple earthen food.

Food unearned by
human deeds, given,
poured out through
the marriage of Spirit and bread.

Countless blessings
planted into a fertile
heart offered in the free
will of a humble servant.

Mystery unto mystery.
Spiritual winds blowing
through the veil of
hope and faith reality.

It is in this reality that
I place my trust, my heart.
I quietly calm my mind,
seeing with eyes of Love.

Praise to the Father.
Praise to the Son,
Glory to Holy Wisdom
Presence, Three in One.

Morning Symphony

Morning symphony.
New day music,
birds glorious song.
We're alive, we're alive.

Quiet mirror face lake.
Veil covering mist,
perhaps the Spirit reflection
moving over morning creation.

Tweets, chirps, tap taps.
Wing splash landings.
Look, look, God is here.
New day, new life expression.

Joyful, peaceful, how can one
ask when we experience God?
Open your ears, open your eyes
to this heaven birth mother.

New sun, new sky,
new air, breathe in
this new day dawning.
New love for all to share.

Come to Me, I Am here.
Listen to My music.
Look at My Earth face.
See My mist spirit giving new life.

See My Cathedral.
Come to My altar of Life.
See My Incarnation.
Listen to My Love-Concert.
Smell My Earth Creation.
Taste the natural bounties.
Touch Me. Feel Me. I Am here.

Keep Watch

Keep watch of the treasures
that take hold of your heart.
Stay connected to your senses,
practicing awareness of the moment,
taking time to appreciate subtle wonders,
allowing time to wander, wonder,
observe, notice, and experience.

Spend time watching clouds move
as they drift artistically across the sky.
Listen to the music of the tall pines,
gracefully at one with the wind.

New Day

The sun's rays dance and skip
along the water's surface,
greeting the morning mist
with the hope of the new day.

Morning offering of the Creator,
giving and emptying,
the Spirit roaming from heart to heart,
Word of God spoken in this new day.

Dance with me oh morning Light.
Sing to me oh Voice of Dawn.
Fill my spirit with the joy of joys,
canticles of praise leaping from my heart.

Moments of this new day approach,
and the sea fog of daily duties
creeps in and eclipses the Light,
ego blindness overtakes true sight.

I will stay awake, heart open,
keeping watch for God-Image,
balancing light and dark with love.
New day, transformation abounds.

Breathing

Nothing breathing.
Empty breathing.
Spirit breathing.
Slow, quiet, present.

Most of the Universe is silent.
No thought.
No ego.
Slow, quiet, present.

Silent praise.
Joined with the Universe.
Open. Awake.
Slow, quiet, present.

No words.
No prayers.
Mirror love.
Soul nourishment.

Swaying

Breathe in the Universe.
Breathe out the Universe.
In a quiet, quiet moment,
Truth touches my heart.

At once I am born again,
alive and awake,
Light shining in my soul,
I was blind, and now I see.

Resurrected from the darkness.
How do I explain the discovery
of what has always been there?
Humility a small price to pay.

Time disappears in the Light,
even if only for moments,
worries and fears are washed
away by beauty and Love.

We are connected through
the reality of Creation,
our simple being connected
with the elements of Eternity.

Hollow Cross

I am like a hollow wooden cross,
made up from small pieces
of (self-offerings) joined together.

I have to work to keep it empty,
open, to allow the Love of God
to fill the inside in order to carry
my cross to the death of my false self,
and the resurrection of my true self,
towards Union with the One.

Capture

You have captured my heart.

Despite struggles,
inside of suffering,
despite distractions,
I hear Your whisper.

Within my busy daily life
You have provided moments.
Among my many weaknesses
You have not gone away.

It is all different now.
I cannot open my eyes
without noticing the Universe.
I am a witness of Your Incarnation.

It is truly different now.
I can never see the world the same.
I have been chosen, set aside,
Wisdom has brushed my cheek.

You have captured my heart.
I willingly surrender to You.
I offer my imperfect efforts.
I offer my silence in moments.

Real Religion

In the little moments,
like waking this morning,
still feeling tired and not
ready for another work day,
my mind far from religion,
in these bare, plain moments,
I think of the distance between
myself and my God.
I think of my lack of ability to
sustain spiritual awareness.

But wait, no, it is different now.
God of the old ways replaced
during my transformation
with the true God of life.
This God is not out there, distant,
but is near me, always with me.
This God of presence, God of reality,
is with me like the air I breathe.
My being, whether consciously or not,
is a dynamic act of God's creative work.
I am religion, an expression of God's creative
sharing of divine life.

A whisper escapes my lips, "Glory".

The gift of grace to realize my
heart is captured now and forever. Amen.

What is Contemplation

Contemplation is putting "self and ego" aside for some moments in order to heart-listen.

As you focus on your breathing in and out, picture the breath flowing past your heart on the way in, and again flowing past your heart on the way out, nourishing with "the essence of Spirit", which is Love.

When in the chapel, picture the breath flowing from the Tabernacle into your lungs and then returning back to the Tabernacle.

When in nature, picture the gentle winds of creation filling your lungs and then returning to it's wonderful source.

Contemplation

Contemplation: getting all the noise and chatter of your mind out of the way so God can speak with your soul.

Spirit Contemplation

"Contemplation is our entering the state of yes". In this state we make our humanity and spirit completely open and available to the presence of the Holy Spirit. We quiet ourselves to all things other than our availability, and we wait.
(Quote attributed to Father Richard Rohr)

God Is.

(Note: Our human mind tries to find a location for God, a place where we can then control the encounter)

All things are in the reality of God.
I'm never separate from God.
Asked by a friend how I experience God,
my simple answer is "I live".
My very "being alive" is an expression
of God's creative Being and Presence.

Every single moment of my life
I'm experiencing God.
It is impossible not to experience God.
I simply wake up and become aware.
I must keep my heart open and available
to this mystical real-moment living.
Even if I'm not mentally or spiritually
engaged with God in the moment,
God is engaged with me.
So, I live with God, live in God, live.

As I move through my days,
I'm ever hopeful for those Grace-filled
moments of spiritual awakening,
when my soul glimpses the unspeakable
Real-ness of the One.

Experience God at all times and rejoice.
Pray always. Your life (your living) is a prayer,
a continuous prayer of your participation
with God in creation.

Perfect Reminder

I am to be small and filled with humility.
I am to be little and filled with love.
I am to be a child of little moments,
traveling along my "move to empty".

I almost lost what You gave to me.
I was looking through my prideful eyes.
My transformation can now continue,
You rescued me from my misdirection.

My misdirection has offered a lesson.
My ego self brought out into the open.
My ego self hiding in fancy words.
My ego self hiding in lofty ideas.

Once again you have pulled back the curtain.
You have made clear my true Lenten gift.
You have shone light into the dark corners of my soul.
You have laid bare my ego pride.

I cannot forget my move to empty.
I cannot allow an ego distraction.
My humility will be my guide forward.
My cross stamped upon my heart.

Let my words be a servant to humility.
Let my actions be a servant to humility.
Let my ego be a servant to humility.
Let my emptiness be a fitting home for humility.

Let me not forget my special purpose.
Let me not forget the journey at hand.
Help me to stay steadfast to the way.
Guide my heart in the way of Compassion.

Little Moments

Little Moments of Love.

Just like when we are awake
and aware of the moments
and glimpses we receive
of the Reality and Presence
of the Creator,
we also need to be aware
of moments of love.
As we move through
our daily lives with our families,
friends, co-workers,
and greater community,
we'll be focused on other things,
other tasks, other duties.
This is when we need
to keep an open heart,
a listening ear,
for these little moments
and opportunities to reflect Love.

Calling

Live quietly.
Live humanly,
Live humbly.
Live with great hope.

Live in the present.
Live in the Presence.
Live in God's expression,
open to moments of love.

Live day by day,
moment by moment,
a humble servant to all,
open to moments of Grace.

Live with quiet joy,
observing without
comment or judgement,
nonviolence as a shield.

Take no offense.
Patience will be both a cross
and a path to transformation.
Empty of all ambitions, except
complete openness and humility.

"Life is not accomplishing some special work but attaining to a
degree of consciousness and inner freedom which is beyond
all works and attainments. That is my real goal. It implies
becoming unknown and as nothing."
(Quote attributed to Thomas Merton)

Thoughts About Trinity

Infinite.
Incarnate.
Intimate.

Our being, our existence, is a dynamic, real, live, expression of the timeless relationship with the Creator. We are an expression of God's Love. The act of creation is an act of relationship. The act of creation is an act of giving and receiving, emptying and filling, loving and accepting love.

Creation is alive and dynamic.
Incarnation is alive and dynamic.
Trinity is alive and dynamic.
Mystery is alive and dynamic.
Trinity is Mystery.

The Infinite is in a relationship with all creation, because all creation is in and part of the Infinite.
We were created for Union with the Infinite. We were created to have a perfect relationship with the Infinite.

Through the Intimate, the Infinite became Incarnate in a special way to have relationship and Union with the created. This is the great Mystery of Trinity. This is our true and holy purpose. We have a special place in creation (created in the image and likeness) with freedom and the gift to know that we know. We are given the freedom to give and receive, to empty and be filled, to love and accept love, or to reject. The Infinite does not force relationship.

The "good news" is that we are offered the amazing gift of experiencing the Kingdom on Earth as it is in Heaven. Remember, Heaven in not a place out there, but a transformation of our being growing in Unity (NOW) with: The Infinite, the Incarnate, and the Intimate.

So here is the most amazing (and important) news. The Infinite, Incarnate, and Intimate is all around us, visible and invisible. Our ability to see (the healing of our blindness) initially comes in small glimpses and moments. That's kind of where I am right now, so I cannot comment much more about what comes next. After all, it is Mystery. I absolutely do know that it will be of the heart, not of the mind. It will be of love, not words. It will be of relationship, not dogma. It will be through selflessness and great humility, not ego. It will be through God's Will, not mine. It will be through Creation Expressions of the relationship of the Infinite, Incarnate, and Intimate, and it will be by our openness and acceptance of God's Love.

Life Actions

A journey from the heart to the world.
Becoming an expression of the being of the Creator.

Life actions. Living moments.
These are moments in our daily lives
in which we witness for God. We receive and we give.
We receive love and we give love.
Expressions. Moments.
We choose to act and share these moments.
This is not a big, flashy religion.
This is simple spirituality.
Living within "Love moments".

We take what has entered into our heart and we share with others, even if in very small ways, small moments. In this way we are not just another clanging cymbal or noisy gong.

More Thoughts About Trinity

Contemplation is the experience of God at our
most basic and simple level.
This is at the level of our "being",
when we have shed everything else,
other than our simplest self, our only real self.

For a moment or perhaps moments, we have silenced ego.
For a moment or perhaps moments,
we have silenced ambitions, hopes, desires, fears, hatreds.
We are just simply present.
We are with I Am.
It is the recognition of Presence.
It is the being of "in-ness".

It is the truth of connectedness, without understanding.
It is the acceptance of Mystery within reality.
Our pure self, with the Infinite,
in the Present Expression Reality,
in a moment of Intimacy, in-ness with Trinity.

Contemplation then is the practice
of glimpsing in-ness with Trinity,
allowing ourselves to be available to Trinity.

This is not limited to times of silence and solitude.
The glimpses can come at anytime,
most easily seen in moments of great love.
They can be noticed while walking, sitting, resting, or working.
However, for most of us, we can notice the best when
we are the least distracted (in the silence, in our night).

Connect

In each morning awakening,
together, as the body,
we greet the sun, the wind,
the waters and the earth,
all creatures, large and small.
one reality, one Universe.
We are co-inhabitants of creation,
all from one Source, one big bang,
all part of the same Expression,
all connected through one Spirit,
one Human-Divine Dance,
many parts, one whole.

We are connected through purpose,
one human race living in harmony
with and within the natural world,
brothers and sisters,
with one Spirit energy of being.
We allow this Spirit to join
with ours, giving and receiving,
emptying and filling,
loving and accepting.
In allowing our purpose to be fulfilled,
our true humanity,
light and energy ripples through the interconnected
systems of a dynamic functioning creation
like tiny waves traveling through space and time
(like our nervous system)
in symbiotic essence, many parts, one whole.

Our expressions are effectual to the health and
well-being of the great functioning creation.
Our participation with the life-energy opens our
pathway to transformational union with the Source of
All as well the great transformation of all things.

Our "being" matters,
our prayers matter,
our openness matters,
allowing the flow of life-energy
within the functioning creation.

New Flow

The flow of creation is like
a wave of energy pulsing,
moving outward and forward,
all things related in one flow,
one energy, one purpose.

Every moment matters,
everything and everyone,
carefully made with intent,
matter and spirit,
matter joined with spirit.
Every moment of our being,
like a living play, participating
in the dynamic Great Plan.
Every moment can be an
awakening to God's presence,
unfolding like a new journey,
connected to the great flow.

The significance of this
is hard to explain.
We are never separate from God,
like ocean waves cannot
be separate from the ocean itself.
Even when our mind or heart
may be very distracted,
God is the I Am, God Is, and we
are the direct expression of Love,
we are the free children of God.

Every moment of your
being is religion.
Your greatest prayer is living.
Your breathing, your walking,
your speaking, your work, your play,
your loving and suffering, all intricate
pieces of the Flow of Creation.

Contemplative Silence

I've become convinced the reason why silence is so important is that you cannot speak without engaging your ego. Even our obsessive thinking is just another way for the ego to talk (on the inside). So, contemplation is about the submission of our ego through silence.

Breathe in, breathe out.
Silence in, silence out.
Silent offering in, silent offering out.

Humor

I believe the Creator has a sense of humor.
We do, so why wouldn't the source of our being.

Sometimes I have to laugh at myself (my ego) during my transformation.

So here in my quiet Chapel, seeking silence, I will be present to the two old men, veterans, and all their whispers, prayers (quiet and loud), noises of canes banging and prayer books rattling, and in this way I'm present to you. Also, to the mother and baby who came to visit, with rattles and coos and bag full of toys, to the baby who is truly the only one here who knows how to be fully present, I will join my energy with theirs in a grand offering of honor and glory.

Container

This feeling of being outside the container (a transcended experience) is perhaps an insight of being outside our false self, the self we initially need to provide the structure of our container.

Temporary Blindness

Where are You?
Where did you go?

Yes, I know, You are here,
You never leave me.
I am in You,
and You are in me,
but I could not find you,
I could not see.

Why do I lose sight?
Why do I get distracted?

I know.
I'll step outside.
It's late, it's night.
A warm night,
star filled black sky.
I walk a little more.

Then I saw them,
there in the scratchy grass,
small but glorious,
little yellow flowers
in the dark of night
gazing upward at the One.

Praise and Glory.
Yes you are here
and I found You
in Your simple creative presence.
I smile, I muse
at Your hello, at Your Love.
Now I can rest,
now I can sleep.
You granted me peace.

Witness

The wind whispers,
the wind calls out,
behold, behold,
take notice, witness
to all the wonders.

Still your mind,
your restless, busy mind.
Slow the motion, feel
the wind brush your skin,
be present to Divine flow.

Living, breathing,
being, in your cells,
in your skin, the warm
sun caressing, sounds
jumping, I Am here, here.

Still your life,
your restless, busy life.
Sharpen your senses,
gifts of nature abound,
sights, sounds, scents.

In every woman, man,
or child, I Am here, here.
In their hearts and souls,
my Spirit moves with
silent gestures and glimpses
of Love manifest for my children.

I long for your notice.
I long for your heart
to receive my reckless love,
Oh, how I desire your heart,
your glance, your knowing.

What else can I do
to win your love?
I've made my grace yours.
My vulnerability is yours.
My complete sacrifice is yours.

I will wait with everlasting mercy.
I will wait with unending patience.
I will be present in all things, all people,
all hearts, all places, in All.
Do you know me? Will you love me?

Gift

The gift, the Grace You have given me,
the gift of awareness of Your Presence,
the gift of Your Promise,
You are with me always.

There was a time when I would wonder,
"Where is my God"?
In my trials,
in my storms, raging storms,
my faith was weak,
my spirit was lost.
Now, You have captured my heart,
You have claimed my spirit,
You have made residence in my soul.
When I was blind and full of myself,
I was blocking my awareness of You.

You have healed me,
You have lifted me up,
You have strengthened me,
Your gift saves me,
Your Grace gives me hope.
Your love for me cannot be extinguished.

Adoration

Reaching Heavenward

A meeting with Divine,
a sacred moment.
In the dark of the night,
in the silent, dark night.

My approach,
calm, so quiet.
Oh world in your sleep,
glimpse the unspoiled Eden.

Stars and moon
watching overhead,
this silent night,
peace lives in these moments.

The heavy wooden doors
swing open giving passage
to the gathering place,
to the moment of encounter.

The gentle flicker of the candles,
the sound of the trickling font,
soft shadows throughout
this humble dwelling.

The lofty ceiling has
collected the prayers
of many longing hearts, openly
waiting for this night's Psalms.

The sturdy wooden pews,
holding the stories of life,
the joys and sorrows,
hopes and dreams of the faithful.

Heaven's Offer

There,
in complete humility,
on a small marble table,
You wait for your people.

Simple bread,
made Holy
by the kiss of
the Holy Spirit.

Divine humility,
greeted by my
humble and
fractured acceptance.

The Litany - My Offering

Glory be to the Father,
the Son,
and the Holy Spirit,
as it is in the night,
in the silence,
in the darkness,
in the Union of the Three
with all things,
now and forever.
I bring to You,
My beating heart.
My emptiness.
My awake-ness.
My presence.
My skin.
My bones.
My breath.
My blood.
My ego.

My weakness.
My drifting mind.
My humanity.
My pride.
My words.
My thoughts.
My dreams.
My empty hands.
My empty basket.
My need for things.
My need for me-ness.
My night.
My silence.
My gaze.
My love.

Here, I can only speak
with my heart,
my only prayer is silence,
my only offering is presence.

Heaven Reaches Forth

And then the moment comes.
I have quieted my words,
my thinking, my agenda.
Finally, I'm truly present.

I've reached contemplation.
The Blessed moment.
A smile of recognition appears.
I cannot hide my joy.

Your Presence,
my presence,
my reality floating
within this Great Incarnation.

For some moments
my spirit becomes free,
separation removed,
open to the infinite.

An expanse so unknown,
unrestricted by physical
boundaries or constraints.
Out of body I suppose.

You have lifted me up.
You have sustained my life.
Undeserved Grace.
Your Love for me is astounding.

This Place

Again the thought of waves,
spiritual waves, for it is
difficult to think or feel
spiritual all the time.
I move throughout my day,
the occasional wave of insight
or inspiration presents itself,
like waves hitting upon
the stubborn shore.

Then, when least expected,
You have taken me
to a mystical place,
a vast ocean of endless Love.
You have saved me from my distress.
You have lifted me out of my prison.
I am humble in your presence.
I am quiet in your gaze.
At this moment I am
empty of myself.
Your inspiration has led
my heart to know that
my move to empty
is not a move to emptiness.
It is a losing, a shedding of
the outer cover, the worldly image,
in order to discover the
true, holy, inner person.

White Room

(Part One)

The inner layer uncovered,
this place has been here always,
waiting from the day of my making.

This place is new to me,
this new discovery.
How does one live more
than half his life without
awareness of his true self?

New life, I'm like an
infant opening his eyes
to a new unfurling world.

Experiencing the inner layer,
the inner self, the inner room,
brilliant light, but at the same time
the unknown, the deep unknown.
Paradox is the way of the One.

I feel a new peace emerging,
a peace based on rising hope.
Move to empty fulfilled with faith.

Now I stand on the precipice
with the understanding that
I've received the greatest of treasures
while simultaneously staring into
the infinity of the Universe.

(Part Two)

I am in all layers at all times.
Three separate layers,
but one being.
For harmony to be maintained,
let not one dominate the others.

Inner layer supporting the two,
physical and projected.
The other two providing
experience of life,
harmony of the whole being.

Contact with the One within all three,
the inner layer providing true unity.
This unity travels in and out like the breath,
touching my world through the physical,
reaching to others through my projection.

Connected to the One in the inner,
therefore, connected through spirit
to all things, all life, all energy.
This, from which I live and breathe
and have my being.

In union with the One of all things,
while remaining a unique creation.
United with brother and sister,
inner light to Inner light to inner light,
deep unto Deep unto deep.

Reminded

Reminded again of humility.
Remember the need for quiet,
for stillness, for waiting.

Understanding will be given
when it is truly needed,
vision will be granted
when sight will open the heart.

Our journey is based upon
the rule of Wisdom, based
on the timeline of eternity.

Truth is truth,
light is light,
we all follow the road
provided by the Spirit-touch.

We are to open our heart
to the whisper of compassion,
witnesses to the Master's work.

We receive the treasures of Grace
while marveling in its beauty.
"The Tao is infinitely illusive,
but at its heart is all being."

Remain as an empty vessel
to be filled with the Spirit of life,
flowing through, reaching out to all.

Rejoice in the mystery of creation.
Take heart from the power within.
Reminded again of humility.
Quiet, still, living with simple joy.

Move To Love

Live within empty,
Move to Love.

Let my empty ego reflect light.
Let my empty ego be filled with love,
then turn and move to give love completely.

I will not desire to possess love,
but to receive love and constantly give love.

Receive light, give light.
Receive love, give love.

No possession, no position,
no self-ambition.

Filling and giving,
filling and giving.

The Way

Opportunities come daily
to learn the lessons of humility.
Our ego is challenged, then we react
based on the level of relationship
of our inner spirit with the great Spirit.

We act and move through our daily lives.
We work, we interact with our brothers
and sisters. If we attach too much importance
to this work, to our performance, creating expectations
based on external worldly values, we will be humbled.
Rather, act and move and work with our spirit centered
on humility. Remain centered not on control, but rather
on openness to the creative force present within us.
Remain focused not on outcomes, but rather
on the reality of our connection with the energy
emanating from our inner life, a life anchored
on the trust and allowance of the living,
guiding Spirit always moving in
the direction of perfecting our human reality.

Not by our control, but by openness
to our inner true self, a self which is
generated from the image of the Divine.
This type of living is contemplation.

The transformation to a life based on
the trust of being centered on our true
inner, Divine image-self is the experience
of new life in the Spirit.

Pray, meditate, focus on allowing this holy transformation to take place in our lives.

We are to accept our humiliations as the acting transformation taking place in our lives.
Learn from them and grow. This is the Creation Action, the Creation Purpose based on the true, ultimate supremacy of the One Life Force.

Living In The Full

We approach our day,
living, breathing, moving,
experiencing the world around us.
We recognize and acknowledge
the Spirit that is in and around and with us.
We are always in the reality of the Great Spirit.

We acknowledge the mystery
of the Spirit and it's dynamic
Creation-work in the world,
acknowledging the unknown
and our lack of understanding,
we accept the present moments
with all their mystery.

We acknowledge and accept
our small role in the Creation-work of Love,
while also knowing our role is cherished by God.
We open ourselves and allow and cooperate
with the flow of Love moving through us.
When we stumble, we move through the actions
of forgiveness, reconciliation, transformation
and reopen ourselves to the flow of Love.

We acknowledge the life we have,
the blood in our veins, the air in our lungs,
the sun on our face, the gentle wind against our cheek.
We offer appreciation and accept stewardship
of the amazing gift of creation.
We let the warmth of Love touch our heart
and put a smile on our face and move
with confidence in the power of Love working in our life.

Acknowledgements

I'd like to take the opportunity to give recognition to a few sources of influence on my writing found throughout this book. Although this work covers a span of 30 plus years of my spiritual journey, the last 4 years have provided significant insight and fulfillment.

I highly enjoy reading the works of great spiritual writers of the past and present. Two authors I'd like to give special recognition to are Thomas Merton and Richard Rohr. I've read many of Thomas Merton's books and am especially attached to his poetry. Richard Rohr continues to be a great spiritual teacher at his Center for Action and Contemplation in Albuquerque New Mexico and has authored many influential books on a broad range of spiritual topics. I cannot recommend highly enough the reading of the works of these two authors. Although my writing is based on my own personal experiences and lifetime events, it would not be hard to recognize the influence these writers have had on my spiritual life. The idea of True Self and False Self which was a vital aspect of Merton's body of work is picked up by Rohr and put into understandable modern writing. I have found a strong connection to this concept and have chosen to include my understanding of this profound Way into my life and writing. Both writers also dive deeply into the concept of the human Ego. My early writing concerning the need for great humility was finally given meaning by my discovery of Merton and Rohr's thorough explanations. My own life experiences have been a strong teacher in the ways of Ego and the crucible of humility. It is these experiences that I try to bring to life in this book.

I'm very thankful to these authors and many others who have made an attempt to bring spiritual enlightenment to those who are searching, no matter what point in their journey. My hope is that in some way this book may bring a similar glimpse into my spiritual growth and perhaps make a difference to those who spend time with my humble words.

I'd like to thank my friends Miss Kyle and Miss Sylvia for encouraging me to make my very personal writings public. As always, I'm very thankful for the love and support from my family and friends.
Bill Huyett

Further reading by Bill Huyett

"Awaken Love"
visit Amazon Books

Made in the USA
Coppell, TX
28 June 2021

58259266R00108